CW00551930

THE WAR EXPERIENCES OF A KOYLI OFFICER
1940–1946

The Author – 1941.
The King's Own Yorkshire Light Infantry.

The War Experiences of a KOYLI Officer 1940–1946

by

J.R.M. Newsome

The Pentland Press Ltd
Edinburgh · Cambridge · Durham · USA

First published in 1998 by
The Pentland Press Ltd.
1 Hutton Close
South Church
Bishop Auckland
Durham

British Library Cataloguing in Publication Data.
A catalogue record for this book is available
from the British Library.

ISBN 1 85821 604 4

Typeset by George Wishart & Associates, Whitley Bay.
Printed and bound by Bookcraft Ltd., Bath.

Contents

Illustrations

Maps

Acknowledgements

*I wish to dedicate this book to my two daughters,
Edina and Elizabeth, as without their gentle persuasion, the
events that took place may never have been recorded.*

*Also my appreciation and thanks to my cousin, Tessa, and her
husband, Dr John Givans, for their guidance and help.*

*My thanks also to Mrs Mary Denton, Publishing Manager,
Mrs Rachel Gowling, Promotions Manager, and all the
staff for their assistance and help in producing this book.*

CHAPTER I

Army Service in the Ranks

After a short leave at home in Dewsbury in 1940, I enlisted at Dewsbury Town Hall, and volunteered for The King's Own Yorkshire Light Infantry. In a few days I received my rail ticket and instructions to report at Strensall Barracks, Nr. York, which was their Regimental Depot. Over the next eight weeks, intensive training took place – weapon training, lectures, map reading – until I was posted to one of their holding units at Hull, and was there helping to guard a barrage balloon station at Sutton, being billetted in Blundells Buildings, an old paint factory near the Station Hotel. I celebrated my twenty-first birthday at home in Dewsbury on leave in the March of that year.

In April I was posted to the 2nd/4th Battalion at Belle Vue Zoo, Manchester. The battalion had recently returned from Cherbourg in France, a fortnight after the evacuation of Dunkirk. After a few months the battalion moved to Hawick in Scotland, and I joined the Intelligence Section at Battalion Headquarters, where I got my first stripe, before being posted to A Company. Hawick was rather a desolate camp, in Nissen huts on the moors, but we were able to visit the town by rail from Hawick Station, when my usual ritual was to have a good bath and a meal at the local hotel twice a week. In the spring of 1940 the battalion moved to St Andrews, Scotland, where our company was under canvas above the golf course, in the grounds of a lovely house, owned by the local laird. By this time I was a full corporal, with my own section, and assisted in the construction of trenches around the golf course, in defence of the coast. I enjoyed my many months in the ranks; it was an experience I shall never forget. I was placed in a rather unusual situation, as some of my closest friends in Dewsbury before the War were commissioned in this battalion, as it was the local Territorial unit, when they joined in 1938. In the early stages I met them off duty in a hotel in Hawick, and then at The Royal & Ancient Hotel at St Andrews, but it must have embarrassed them from time to time as I was a corporal, and, eventually, this had to cease by order of the Commanding Officer – quite right!

The Germans had now reached the Channel Coast in May 1940. I remained with the battalion at St Andrews from June to September 1940, and was there during the Battle of Britain in August/September. We continued our training during that beautiful summer, on full alert in order to man the trenches, as we were expecting an invasion by the Germans, which could have been on this coast. We did many exercises in the area – lovely countryside – which enabled us to enjoy the training. A local baker's van visited the company twice a week, and I enjoyed the lovely cakes available for sale, a nice luxury which I was able to have from the extra bit of pocket money my mother sent to me each week, whenever she returned my clean washing! I sent my dirty washing to her every week whilst I was in the ranks; I also enjoyed my visits twice a week to one of the local hotels with a friend, where I had a bath and a meal, then on to the Red Cross Centre.

CHAPTER II

168 OCTU at Droitwich – Commissioned as a 2/Lt in KOYLI

In November 1940 I was recommended for a commission and posted to 168 OCTU at Droitwich. It was a great experience serving in the ranks – I found the men to be the 'salt of the earth', with a great sense of humour and loyalty – and I was sorry in some ways to leave them. They gave me a great send-off and the Company Sergeant Major, when I said goodbye to him, found some excuse to shout at me in the office before I left, with a twinkle in his eye!

I travelled by train from St Andrews. Most of the hotels had been taken over as accommodation for the cadets, who all wore white bands on their caps. During the next six weeks we were subjected to extensive training and exercises night and day, and were made familiar with the duties and responsibilities of an officer, until I was commissioned just before Christmas in December 1940. I had volunteered for the KOYLI and it was with a feeling of much pride that I learnt that I had passed, and ordered my uniform from a local shop, to arrive home for Christmas as a Second Lieutenant in the same regiment as my grandfather (Major T.H. Newsome TD VD), who had also served in the 1st Battalion, as a Territorial officer, before the First World War. I had about a week's leave, and was then posted to the battalion stationed at Rochdale.

At the outbreak of the War, the 1st Battalion was at Strensall,

York, and in October 1939 left for France as one of the units of 15 Brigade, part of the 5th British Division, with whom it remained throughout the War. After some months of 'phoney war', and a rapid move at short notice, the battalion sailed from Rosyth for Norway, and landed at Andalsnes in April 1940. It fought its first action of the War, and earned the battle honour of 'Kvan', but retreat was inevitable, and late at night on 1 May it re-embarked and left for home in the small hours of the 2nd. After a period of leave and reorganization, the battalion spent the rest of the summer and autumn in Scotland and moved to winter quarters at Rochdale at the end of October.

It was from now on that my experiences as a commissioned officer commenced and little did I know then that it was to take me to many interesting countries in the Far East, Middle East and Europe.

I reported to the Adjutant of the battalion at Rochdale in January 1941.

Infantry Order of Battle, 1943–1945

8th ARMY (Montgomery)

XXX Corps	XIII Corps
(Lieutenant General Leese)	(Lieutenant General M.C. Dempsey)
51st Highland Division	50th British Division & Commandos
1st Canadian Division & Commandos	
	5th British Division (Major General H.F.M. Berney Fickling) & Commandos
231 Brigade	13 Infantry Brigade 2nd Cameronians 2nd Inniskillins (until July 1944)

5th Essex (from July 1944)
2nd Wilts
91st Field Regiment RA
   (London Territorial)
157 Field Ambulance
7th Cheshires (Machine-Gun
   Battalion)
15 Infantry Brigade
(Brigadier G.S. Rawstone)
1st Bn Green Howards
1st Bn KOYLI
1st Bn York & Lancasters
92nd Field Regiment RA
7th Cheshires
158 Field Ambulance
17 Infantry Brigade
2nd Royal Scot Fusiliers
2nd Northants
2nd Seaforth Highlanders
93rd Field Regiment RA
7th Cheshires
159 Field Ambulance
Armoured regiment supporting
   us in Sicily was 3rd County
   of London Yeomanry

I have endeavoured to relate these events as accurately as possible, together with press releases, but apologize for any errors which may have occurred, and for any other points of interest not mentioned, which happened over fifty years ago.

I was known as 'Jumbo' in the battalion and the Regiment, and am still referred to by this nickname.

5

CHAPTER III

History of the King's Own Yorkshire Light Infantry

The Regiment was raised in 1755 in the Leeds area. Four years later on 1 August 1759, the 51st Foot, as it was then known, was one of six regiments of British Infantry which totally defeated the French Cavalry at the Battle of Minden. Since then units of the Regiment have served and fought all over the world, from Iceland to Tasmania, from Hong Kong to South Africa.

The KOYLI has seen many changes in its history, one of the most far reaching being in 1881 when the British Army was reorganized and the 51st became the 1st Battalion The King's Own Light Infantry (South Yorkshire Regiment). At the same time the 2nd Regular Battalion was formed from the 105th Madras European Light Infantry, and the West Yorkshire Militia became the 3rd (Militia) Battalion. Later, two territorial Army Battalions, the 4th (Wakefield) and 5th (Doncaster) were included, and the Regimental Depot was established at Pontefract.

In common with the rest of the Army the Regiment expanded considerably in the First World War when no less than twenty-six Battalions saw service in all major theatres. In the Second World War, the 1st, 1/4th and 2/4th Battalions fought in the European theatres; the 2nd Battalion was decimated in the first Burma campaign and remained in the Far East for the rest of the War; and the 5th Battalion converted into two Regiments of Artillery.

In 1948 the 1st and 2nd Battalions were amalgamated, and since then the 51st/105th has seen little service at home. The battalion fought the communists in Malaya, the Mau-Mau in Kenya, the EOKA in Cyprus, the Indonesians in Borneo and the terrorists in Aden. Interspersed with these campaigns, the battalion has also served in relatively peaceful stations in Germany, Malaya, Berlin and at Tidworth.

CHAPTER IV

Brigadier E.E.E. Cass CBE DSO MC, Commanding Officer 1st Bn, 1940–1942

He was the Commanding Officer of the battalion when I joined them at Rochdale. All of us had a very high respect for him. He was gazetted 2nd Lt in 1916 and served with distinction in the First World War, being awarded the MC and DSO.

Between the two wars, 'Copper' made his name as a rugby player and shot. He led the 1st Battalion Rugby team in winning the Rhine Army Rugby Cup and played for the Army for several years.

His skill as a shot was soon recognized – he was a member of the Army Eight, and was in the King's 100 every year from 1922–30. He won a number of cups and was posted to the 2nd Battalion in 1934.

In 1935 he won the British Army Championship in India and was second in the Revolver Cup. He was seconded as an Instructor to the Indian Small Arms School and won The King's Medal in 1936.

At the start of the Second World War he was second in command of the 1st Battalion and assumed command in Norway. His handling of the 1st Battalion during this short campaign was masterly. The chapter in Vol V of the Regimental History was shown to the C-in-C, General Sir Bernard Paget, who wrote, 'You ask if you have praised the KOYLI too highly for their part in the campaign; you are not too strong in your praise. The battalion fought splendidly under the inspiring leadership of Cass, and, of him, I would say that there is no one I would sooner have with me in a tight place.'

Lieutenant Colonel Cass was given the immediate award of a bar to his DSO. He commanded the battalion until February 1942, shortly after we had left Northern Ireland, and there is no doubt that the standard of discipline and training that he instilled into the battalion lasted for the rest of the War – few of us who were in the battalion at the time will ever forget him.

I remember, in Northern Ireland, he gave instructions for all subalterns to be on parade at 6 a.m. every morning for PT under the PT Sergeant. Although most of us moaned about it, especially at that hour, there is no doubt that it enabled us to be extremely fit. On a number of occasions, as the battalion was on parade for a twelve-mile route march, which took place once a week, he walked onto the parade ground just before we were about to set off, and ordered all ranks to take off their equipment and lay it on the ground, in order to inspect the items in the haversack. There were a number of items missing, thus reducing the weight in the pack. The parade was dismissed by the Adjutant and all had to return to their huts in order to have the correct items in the haversack. This delayed the route march by some two hours, which meant we did not return to camp until 8 p.m., too late for any sporting activities that had been arranged, as well as visiting the town, and the men's feet had to be inspected first. This taught us a lesson for the future. The Adjutant had all subalterns on parade, and give us a good telling off because we had not inspected our platoons properly. On these long route marches, 'Copper' would park his vehicle down a lane after we had marched about eight miles and survey us all as we passed, to ensure that we were marching properly with our weapons. On a number of occasions he caught the officers carrying the anti-tank gun (which was quite heavy after all those miles) in order to give the men a break, but later, these officers were brought in front of him in his office and given a real dressing down. I was caught once or twice, but these incidents and others under his leadership served to toughen us up and certainly we became a very fit unit.

He left us after we had returned from Northern Ireland and commanded 11 Brigade in the First Army Assault on North Africa and in Italy. He was brought home for the landing in Normandy, commanded 8 Brigade in the assault and was wounded in October 1944. On return from hospital he commanded 183 Infantry Brigade and later 114 Infantry Brigade. He was created CBE and received the US Silver Star.

After the war he spent several years as Secretary of the Army Rifle Association and retired to near Scarborough. I met him on two occasions after the War when we attended the 1st Battalion reunion at Leeds every March. He died in about 1980, and is buried at Scarborough.

CHAPTER V

Three Generations – 1941

Three generations in service uniform – 1941.
L to R. Lt. J.R.M. Newsome, Major T.H. Newsome TD VD,
Flt. Lt. T.H. Newsome (Junior)

This photograph was taken at our home 'Longlands', Halifax Road, Dewsbury, Yorks. when my father and I were on leave. My grandfather had kept his uniform from his Territorial years, and brought it out especially for the occasion. It featured in both Dewsbury papers at the time.

My grandfather was also in the 1st Battalion King's Own

Yorkshire Light Infantry, and served with the battalion without a break for twenty years, as a Territorial officer. It was afterwards known as the 4th Battalion KOYLI. He retired in 1908 with the rank of Major, and occupied the office of Major Staff Officer in the Brigade for seven years. When the First World War broke out he immediately answered a request to rejoin the forces and became the Chief Recruiting Officer for the West Riding of Yorkshire. Since he took charge, about 1,000 men were enlisted through his office up to June 1915. He died in 1945, aged seventy-six.

My father was in the Royal Flying Corps in the First World War as a Fighter Pilot, and was also an instructor at a southern Flying School. He was awarded the Croix du Guerre for rescuing a French pilot who had been shot down. In 1939 he formed the first Dewsbury Air Defence Cadets Squadron (No. 96) in January of that year, before he volunteered for the RAF when war broke out in September. He was in Radar Operations, and became Officer Commanding a Radar Station at Staxton, near Scarborough, Yorks. He died in 1984 aged eighty-nine.

I served with the King's Own Yorkshire Light Infantry throughout the War, rising from the ranks to Captain, and was captured in Sicily by the Hermann Goering Parachute Division in July 1943, spending the rest of the War as a POW in Italy and Germany, until I was repatriated from Germany in 1945. I was demobilized in 1946.

CHAPTER VI

Rochdale and Northern Ireland

The commemoration of Minden Day – the Regiment's first battle honour – in August 1759, is celebrated every year, when white roses are worn by all ranks on their headdresses. The other five regiments of British Infantry which commemorate Minden Day follow the same custom.

Regimental Pride

Weekly on Band Nights in the Officers' Mess the senior officer, after the Sovereign's Toast has been drunk, proposes a second toast to 'Dyas and the Stormers', which is also drunk by all present, standing up and in silence.

Ensign Joseph Dyas led the 'Forlorn Hope' (as the leading echelon of any storming party on a fortress was called) in the assault on the massive walls of Badajoz in 1811, during the Peninsular War. It was found that the scaling ladders were six feet too short. In spite of intense enemy fire, which filled the ditch below the wall with dead and dying, Dyas reorganized his party and tried three times to scale the wall. His cap was blown off his head and his sword shot out of his hand.

Some days later a further assault was ordered, and again Dyas volunteered to lead saying, 'If you order the fort to be stormed forty times, I am determined to lead the advance as long as I have life.' They were prominent in Wellington's unsuccessful attempt to take the fortress in 1811 whereas they were not among the regiments engaged when eventually the fortress fell to the British in the following year.

The Regiment does not bear Badajoz on its colours and has a justifiable grievance in not being allowed to do so. Yet the unsuccessful assault in 1811 left to the 51st one of its heroes and also one of its most lovingly cherished traditions in the person of Ensign Joseph Dyas and his 'forlorn hope' who led the storming parties three times, which were only repulsed after heavy fighting and with grievous losses.

There were in those days no decorations for bravery in the field, but, in consideration of Dyas's heroism, Wellington offered him a Lieutenancy in any corps of the Army which he chose to name. Fortunately for Dyas there was an immediate vacancy in the 51st in place of a subaltern of the Regiment who was mortally wounded, and Dyas continued and eventually completed his service in his own regiment. A greater and more permanent honour awaited him, and he is still remembered in his regiment when its officers dine in mess on band nights. The *Naval and Military Gazette* for 1850 records that Dyas was, during his military career, considered to be one of the bravest officers of any grade in the British Army. He frequently volunteered his services for the most arduous and hazardous duties and 'Dyas and the Stormers' was a standing toast of the most distinguished campaigners of the day. The toast was revived in the 1st Battalion the King's Own Yorkshire Light Infantry about 1908, and the privilege of honouring this toast was later extended to the 2nd and 3rd (Militia) Battalions and, after the First World War, to the two Territorial battalions, the 4th and 5th Battalions KOYLI.

The battalion was billeted in a number of factory buildings in the area of the Rochdale Public Swimming Baths, with the exception of one company which was stationed at Littleborough. During this period we carried out the usual training exercises, route marches, rifle range practice on the moors and battalion parades on Rochdale Football Ground. The local people were extremely friendly, and many marriages resulted from our presence here.

Minden Day, August 1941 – Baron's Court, Co. Tyrone, Northern Ireland. L. to R. Mary Martelli, Jack Newsome, Andrew Young, Topper Topliss, Mary Martelli's brother, Michael Elcomb, Oscar Scargill. Mr Martelli was Bailiff for Lord Brookborough's estate. He and his wife and daughter and son were invited as guests.

In early April 1941, we crossed over to Northern Ireland, via Larne and Stranraer, then proceeded by train to Newton Stewart, near Armagh, where we remained for a few weeks, then we spent the summer under canvas at Barons Court, Lord Brookborough's estate – the residence of the Prime Minister of Northern Ireland. This was a beautiful estate, with a large lake. The battalion parades were held on the vast lawn in front of his very impressive mansion. It was from here that I went to Dublin (in civilian clothes) with two friends for a short weekend, and enjoyed the experience of the bright lights again, as there was no blackout. Good food,

Northern Ireland – 1941. D Company Platoon Commanders –
Ted Simpson (killed 12/1/44), Jack Newsome, Walter Dew.

chocolates, and silk stockings to take home! We were continually
on the alert for the IRA and all other ranks had to sleep with their
rifles by their bedside. In the autumn we moved to winter quarters
at Omagh, in Nissen huts, a nice town where we spent many happy
hours off duty in the evenings. We continued our intensive training,
with long weekly route marches, and many brigade and divisional
exercises by day and night.

In January 1942 we returned to the United Kingdom and were

Northern Ireland – 1941. A.N. Other, R.G. (Gilly) Gillibrand,
Jack Newsome, Jack Bousefield, Barny Pryer.

billetted in houses in the area of Sutton, Surrey. It was here, over
the next few weeks, we were issued with tropical uniform, so we
became aware that we were shortly about to go abroad. I
particularly recall spending a night out in London, and catching the
last train back from Waterloo. As I was looking at the engine, the
driver approached me and said, 'Would you like to travel with me
in the cab? Jump in quickly – this is my little war effort for you
boys.' It was quite an experience in the blackout, and each time we
approached a station I had to disappear to the back of his cab, as,
of course, it was against regulations to do this kind of thing. As a
young boy I always wanted to be an engine driver, and at that time
had quite a large collection of Hornby trains which were frequently
laid out, with all the rails, on the landing at my home, much to the
irritation of my parents, so this incident was the nearest I ever got
to being a train driver! A few days before we left by train for
Liverpool, the whole Brigade was inspected by the then Duke of
Gloucester on Epsom racecourse.

CHAPTER VII

Departure from the United Kingdom – Invasion of Madagascar

On 16 March 1942, we travelled by train to Liverpool and then embarked on the Cunard Liner *Samaria* which was on the quayside by the Liver Buildings, before we sailed for Glasgow, where the convoy was assembled before departing from the Clyde on 23 March, my birthday. At that time, we were the largest convoy ever to have sailed from the United Kingdom, via The Cape, with an escort of an aircraft carrier, cruiser, and six destroyers – a very impressive array when we got under way, with the destroyers on the horizon, and the aircraft carrier with its planes continually flying around the ships. It was a long and monotonous voyage, travelling at 6 knots, and constantly changing course at the sound of the ship's sirens, but, fortunately we were not attacked at any time during the journey. We had Bofors guns on the liner to defend us from air attacks, and target practice took place frequently during the day, which added to our interest. Our accommodation was very cramped, and we were restricted in what we could do, but managed PT on the deck to keep fairly fit. We called at Freetown and Mombassa, but were not allowed ashore, and crossed the Equator in the traditional style, with plenty of activities in the swimming pool, which kept us amused. The weather became so hot that I was unable to sleep in my cabin – there were six of us in bunks – and each night I went up onto the Promenade Deck and slept on my mattress. The deck was usually swilled down at 6 a.m. so I had to be up, but it was worth it, even if the breeze was warm. The convoy was now split up and was considerably reduced with only the cruiser as an escort, as the threat of an attack had receded. Our brigade (15th) spent three days at Cape Town, and I had an enjoyable day ashore with friends, wandering around the town and lunch at the Del Monico Hotel, enjoying the Cape brandy! A considerable number of civilian cars were on the quayside, and the residents took some of the officers and men to their homes for a meal and a journey around the town. The rest of the convoy, containing 13 and 17 Brigades, the other two in the 5th British Division, had sailed direct to Durban, and it was from there that they took part in the landing on Madagascar, the first of the allied invasions on 5 May. We took no part in this, and sailed to Bombay, arriving there on 21 May 1942. The Japanese raids on Ceylon had increased Allied fears that the Axis forces might use Madagascar as a base from which to cut their supply line round the Cape of Good Hope, for the island had remained loyal to the Vichy regime after the fall of France.

In 1942 all British supplies and reinforcements to the Middle East and India had to move via the Cape of Good Hope, then pass along one side or other of Madagascar, on their way north or north-east. If Japanese or German submarines had been able to operate from Diego Suarez north of the island, they would have been able to close both routes, throttling both the build-up in Egypt against Rommel, and that in India against the Japanese.

The invasion force for Madagascar had originally been assembled to forestall any German moves against Spain, the Azores, or the Canaries during late 1940 and 1941, but it was allowed to continue training and working up when no such moves occurred. The target finally selected was the Vichy French base of Diego Suarez, and as the Expeditionary Force sailed the invasion was also an invaluable training exercise in the transport of amphibious forces.

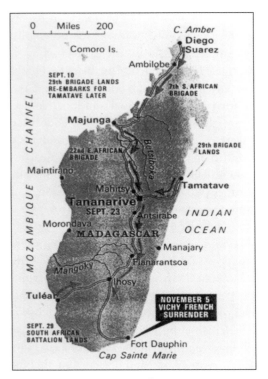

Map 1 – Madagascar.

In February 1942 General Smuts telegraphed Churchill that he looked upon Madagascar as the key to the defence of the Indian Ocean, and reminded him that the Vichy French had allowed the Japanese into Indo-China without resistance or protest. On 12 March Churchill told the Chiefs of Staff to study the problem of an invasion of Madagascar again and with urgency, and on the 14th he telegraphed Roosevelt that a force was to be despatched covered by ships of Force H from Gibraltar, thus leaving the Eastern Fleet free to face the Japanese.

Reaching the War Office early on 14 March 1942, General

Sturgess, Royal Marines, was told of the decision to seize Diego Suarez. In the interests of speed and economy of shipping, his earlier Operation Bonus plan was to be radically altered. The 5th Infantry Division was already embarking at Liverpool for passage to India as Convoy WS-17, but it had no amphibious training and was not embarked for an opposed landing, moreover, its brigade groups were in separate groups of ships. From it General Sturgess would be given 17 Infantry Brigade commanded by Brigadier G.W.B. Tarleton; to this would be added Brigadier F.W. Festing's 29 Independent Brigade Group (which had been placed under Sturgess's command for the Canary Islands operation and was now fully trained in amphibious warfare) and No. 5 Commando. As the force rounded the Cape of Good Hope, orders came from London adding a second Brigade Group, 13 Brigade, to the force – from the 5th Division – but with most of its men in one large vulnerable liner, the *Franconia*, completely untrained in amphibious matters, and not due at Durban until 29 April, this Brigade Group promised to be more of an embarrassment than a help. Yet it would have taken a bold man to query the order, clearly inspired by Churchill himself; a few days later 13 Infantry Brigade, which had followed the 17th ashore, embarked for India, and early in June the 17th followed it on relief by 22 East African Brigade. After our two brigades had landed in the north of the island on 5 May, it was not until 5 November that the Vichy French surrendered the whole island.

The landings at Diego Suarez were not enough – further operations were needed to secure the island. The key zone of the campaign was at this port and Antsirane, across the water. The landings went well although they were jeopardized by fierce enemy resistance at Antsirane, but by 7 May the port had fallen. The northern bases on Madagascar were in Allied hands, and all that remained was to consolidate the spoils, though malaria was to claim many lives.

21

CHAPTER VIII

Overseas Service in India, Persia & the Middle East

In the meantime, we had arrived at Bombay, and spent a short time in a transit camp at Poona; we took advantage of using the swimming pool there, as well as visiting Bombay. A very impressive sight was enjoying tea on the balcony of the Taj Mahal Hotel, which overlooked the sea, and observing the Indian women walking on the promenade, displaying all their beautiful coloured dresses. It was a lovely sight. In early June the battalion entrained for a journey through the Central Provinces to Ranchi, in the North. It was an extremely hot journey, but I was fortunate enough to be the officer in charge of the allocation of the ice to the companies! We picked up the ice from various stations on route, about every five hours. I shall always remember this journey, as I travelled for a number of hours with the engine driver in his cab, and saw some beautiful countryside, many paddy fields; but there was much poverty in the country. This was most noticeable after we had landed, with beggars everywhere and continually harassing you. We eventually arrived at Ranchi, and were encamped under canvas some two miles from the town. Ranchi was quite a pleasant small Indian town, but there was little of interest for us there. As I was responsible for supplying extra items for the Officers' Mess, namely bread, cakes and confectionery, transport was provided for me, enabling me to purchase from the shops. I became friendly with an Indian who owned a bakery, and he kindly gave me an iced cake once a week in appreciation of the business I gave him! Needless to say the cake had to be eaten within two days, which presented no problem to myself and friends! Mosquito nets were standard equipment, and because of the heat, we commenced training at 5 a.m. The siesta was from 1 p.m. to 3 p.m. We got accustomed to the continual noise of the frogs! During this period we were training for jungle warfare until August, and then we returned back to Bombay to begin another journey by boat to Basra, via the Persian Gulf. We remained in a transit camp here under canvas for a few days before departing by road to Qum, in Persia, via Kermanshah.

It was an interesting voyage up the Shat-al-Arab, passing the oilfields by the river bank, at Abadan, until we arrived at Basra, a very bleak and hot area, barren and uninteresting. It was an uncomfortable three days here under canvas, hardly able to do anything because of the heat, and the scorpions gave us much trouble; we were pleased to get under way again and to move by road to Qum, experiencing desert-like country, with occasional small villages, and little or no vegetation. The whole Division was encamped in this area, under canvas, and some three miles from the Holy City itself. As it was extremely cold at night, all the tents were dug underground, with just the tops showing; the subalterns had small tents, which were just able to take a camp bed and about three feet more space. At night-time we heated our tents with charcoal, which was burnt in large tins with an open-cut front, and a chimney protruding out of the tent. In this way we were able to keep our sleeping quarters warm at night, as the temperature used to drop well below freezing, and it was very cold. The night exercises were pretty grim. There was a marked contrast during the day, when it was very hot. It was not a pleasant country to be stationed in, but we made the best of it during our off-duty hours, with football, basketball, and cockfighting, which provided enough interest to keep ourselves from getting too bored. I spent a day in Tehran, some sixty miles north, which was interesting. Our period of stay in Persia was for four months before we departed for the Lebanon.

Officer friends in the Middle East – 1943.

Our regular 5th Division was now known as 'The Globe Trotters' because we were held in reserve to combat any threat by the Japanese in the Far East and by the Germans to any theatre of war in Europe. We were sent to India should the Japanese break through from Burma in 1942, and when this threat was averted we were sent to Persia to defend the oilfields should the Germans break through the Caucasus, but when this was also averted we were sent by road to the Middle East. It was a long journey and a hot one from Qum in December 1942, with a one-night stop at a transit camp at Baghdad, before we arrived at Nathania, south of Haifa in Palestine. This was a pleasant three-day stay in another transit camp under canvas – the country was beautiful in marked contrast to our previous station, with grapefruits and oranges off the trees and a lovely climate. One or two officers were able to visit Jerusalem for the day.

The next stage of our journey took us by road to the Lebanon in early December, and our battalion encamped in a lovely little spot in the hills in Nissen huts – the spring flowers were lovely. It was here that we really commenced our Combined Operational Training, practicing on the ground the procedure for disembarking off landing craft, and a considerable number of exercises took place. I spent a pleasant day and evening with some friends in Beirut, attending a night club in the evening and dancing with the club girls.

Perhaps it might be amusing to recall that when we went to this night club in Beirut, after we had had a number of dances and drinks, I was somewhat annoyed that my hostess was not drinking the alcohol that I had paid for, and that it was just coloured water. I drew her attention to it remarking, 'I do not like wasting my money, please have a decent drink.' Whereupon she burst into tears and left me on my own at the table, where I remained for the rest of the evening! My friends continued to dance with their partners, but no girls ventured to dance with me! Obviously the word had been passed around. We had a good laugh about it – I might have saved money, but missed a little pleasure!

As the weeks went by there was no doubt that our training was building up to something on a large scale, and this was confirmed when we had orders to move to the Suez Canal in March 1943; whilst there we did further training on the Canal with the use of landing craft. Whilst training, one of our companies had a tragic accident whilst practising crossing the Canal with live ammunition. A mortar bomb exploded on a landing craft on an exercise on 1 April, killing two officers and six other ranks. I was one of the bearers of the coffin of the subaltern when they were all buried in the army cemetery in the area. It was very hot training there, but we were able to have the facility of the bathing pool on the Canal. I remember and ENSA concern entertaining us in the open air, by the side of the Canal and Beatrice Lilley was one of the stars!

It was now time to embark on HMT *Reina de Pacifico* and having accomplished this on the quayside at Suez, we took part in a dress rehearsal up the Gulf of Aqaba, which is the next gulf to Suez. No troops landed in this barren area as it was then (although it is now, I believe, a thriving port) as the exercise was for the ships in our convoy. We returned to anchor in the Canal area for a couple of days before we set sail from Port Said on 5 July 1943, and it was from there on that we were informed that we were to invade Sicily. When we knew our destination, there was a mixed feeling of excitement and relief, and a certain amount of tension knowing full well that we were liable to be attacked from the air or sea before we ever reached Sicily.

Since everything which happened in Italy during the first six months of 1943 stemmed from some action by the Allies – the capture of Tunis, the assault on Sicily, the bombing of Rome – it is vital to understand Allied strategy in the Mediterranean.

At the Casablanca conference on 23 January 1943, the British and Americans disagreed on their strategy for Italy. The British plan was to keep the Germans fighting hard in the Mediterranean during the many months which must elapse before the Allies could make their main attack on the Continent, across the English Channel. They therefore proposed that the invasion of Sicily should be a stepping-stone to the Italian mainland, hoping to draw Hitler into a major campaign in the Mediterranean, and compel him to reinforce the defence of Southern Europe at the expense of France and the Low Countries. The assault on Italy might also cause the fall of Mussolini, with serious repercussions on the other German alliances. Moreover, bases in Italy would facilitate the bombing of German war factories and, equally important, the Rumanian oilfields.

The Americans were strongly opposed to this; General Marshall feared the creation in Italy of a vacuum into which the resources of the cross-channel (English Channel) operation would be dissipated – just as the Germans had bled themselves to death in the North African Campaign. As Churchill wrote: 'The Americans believed the Germans would withdraw in Italy, and we would be hitting air.' Any excess forces not required for the English Channel operation should be employed against Japan. In view of American responsibility in the Far East, this was understandable.

The American and British conceptions of warfare were also different. The Americans approached it in the characteristic, forthright manner of a people possessing unlimited resources, anxious to get it over as soon as possible. Who was the main enemy? Germany – where could it be destroyed most quickly? Across the English Channel. Then everything should be devoted to that end and if existing forces were insufficient for it, they should be built up until they were overwhelmingly sufficient.

The British possessed neither the men nor the industrial power to view it in this light. Britain's aim has always been, as a sea power, to avoid head-on collisions, to weaken the enemy by oblique approach. The Americans wanted to outproduce Hitler, the British wanted to outmanoeuvre him.

After much argument at Casablanca, the Americans admitted grudgingly that, if some sort of invasion of the European mainland were not staged for 1943 (the cross-channel operation being out of the question in that year) the Russians might well come to terms with Hitler, as they had in 1939. They therefore agreed to the invasion of Sicily, but no far-reaching plans were made for a further attack on the mainland. It was only with the fall of Mussolini while the Sicilian operation was in progress – making the argument for invasion of Italy seem overwhelming – that Operation 'Avalanche' (attack around the Naples area) was considered. And by then much American shipping had already been withdrawn to other theatres of war.

A further source of disagreement between the Allies was the unconditional surrender call which was Roosevelt's idea. Had it been differently phrased for Italy, Mussolini might well have paid some attention to it. But this demand, together with the Allies' propaganda attempts to divide him from the Italian people, representing him as the sole agent of their disasters, only threw him further into the arms of Hitler. Churchill was in favour of treating Italy differently from Germany. (It is probable that he was finally persuaded to agree with Roosevelt by his British colleagues, who feared that more lenient treatment for Italy would antagonize their Balkan allies, Greece and Yugoslavia.)

A final important part of Allied Mediterranean strategy once the invasion of Sicily had been agreed upon was Operation 'Mincemeat'. On 9 May 1943, the corpse of a British officer was found washed up on the coast of Southern Spain and attached to his wrist was a briefcase containing the Allied order of battle for the invasion of Italy. The Spanish authorities handed this over to the Germans, who learned from it that the Allied invasion was to start in Sardinia, combined with a feint attack on Sicily. To the German General Staff this was logical – the Allies would then try to invade the north of Italy from the Gulf of Genoa. The notion that they would work their way up a mountainous peninsula favourable to the defenders, punctuating the advance by tactical landings of little political importance or operational value, seemed highly unlikely – and Operation 'Mincemeat' confirmed this diagnosis.

When Mussolini informed Hitler that he was concerned about

an invasion of Sicily, the Führer disagreed. Indeed, Hitler now gave express instructions that measures for the defence of Sardinia and Northern Italy were to take precedence over everything else in the Mediterranean theatre.

There is no doubt that Operation 'Mincemeat' had a great bearing on the unopposed landings on the beaches, as we were able to regroup immediately without any counter-attacks before proceeding inland for about half a mile, when we first met Italian opposition. It was only when the Germans realized what was happening that the opposition became much stiffer when we came up against them.

CHAPTER IX

Sicily – The Assault

From mid-January to mid-June, Allied naval and military staffs were wrestling with the gigantic problems of putting eight divisions simultaneously ashore on an enemy-held coastline – the largest amphibious assault ever planned. Not only was the size of the operation unprecedented, but on the eve of the attack a freak storm threatened to wreck everything.

The key objective of the invasion of Sicily was the town of Messina on the north-east corner of the island, for its possession would cut off the flow of German and Italian reinforcements from the Italian mainland only 2 miles away across the narrowest part of the straits. Despite the importance of Messina, however, there could be no question of an immediate attack upon it, for it was outside the range of Allied fighters, whose cover would be essential for the success of the operation. But if the Allied air umbrella would not stretch as far as Messina it would, from its bases on Malta, Gozo, and in North Africa, cover the southern coast of Sicily, which would serve as a stepping stone on the way to Messina, with the nearby ports of Palermo, Syracuse, and Catania.

These places would be the first objectives of the landing, but even with air cover it would be impossible to make a head-on attack against any of them. The experience of the British and the Canadians at Dieppe and of the Americans at Oran had shown that a direct attack from the sea against any defended port would generally be unsuccessful and always costly, for it meant tackling the enemy where he was strongest – against heavy guns, mines in the sea or ashore, barbed wire, anti-tank obstacles, and troops well dug in. Accordingly it had been decided that future attacks upon ports were to be made by troops landing on beaches out of range of the post defences. When the troops were ashore they would fight their way overland to take the port from the flank or the rear. This phase of the operation had to be completed very rapidly, for it would not be possible to keep the armies ashore supplied with heavy material over the beaches. Deep-water quays, cranes, good roads, and the rest of the paraphernalia of a seaport would be necessary.

In fact, after the operation had begun, it was found that much more was possible in the way of supply over the beaches than had been thought possible. This was thanks to the introduction of a new means of amphibious transport known as the DUKW, or Duck, which was a small self-propelled lighter in the sea and a medium-sized truck ashore. (The initials of its name stood for the makers code – D for year of origin, the fourth of the war, U for Utility, K for front-wheel drive, W for six-wheeled.)

To help establish the troops ashore support would be provided by six British battleships: *Nelson*, *Rodney*, *Warspite*, *Valiant*, *Howe*, and *King George V*. The first four were to bombard enemy positions ashore, while the last two were held in reserve in case the Italian battle fleet came out. Before the operation began the Americans were doubtful of the need for this support, but the British, with the experience of Dieppe (where there had been no heavy guns in support) behind them, felt that they knew better.

The first plan for the landing called for an American attack near Palermo and an Anglo-Canadian attack near Catania, the two attacks thus being separated by the length of the island.

But Montgomery, commanding the Anglo-Canadian 8th Army, reacted violently against this to Alexander, who was the military Commander-in-Chief of both the 8th Army and the US 7th Army under General Patton. On 24 April he wrote: 'Planning so far has been based on the assumption that the opposition will be slight and that Sicily will be captured relatively easily. Never was there a greater error. The Germans and also the Italians are fighting desperately now in Tunisia and will do so in Sicily.' Montgomery proved to be overcautious but his army was the only one that Britain had for operations in Europe and it was faced by an unprecedented task. Consideration was given to the objections by Montgomery and the whole plan was recast.

After the War Cunningham said that from the naval point of view the original plan would have worked. But as he wrote: 'It has to be realized that any amphibious operation is merely the opening, under particular circumstances, of a primarily army battle. It is the function of the navy and the air force to establish a base or bases on the hostile coast from which the military tactical battle must be developed to gain the final object.'

But to do that the air force also had to have its say, and for 'Husky' their first concern was the number of airfields concentrated in the south and south-west of Mt. Etna. These had to be out of enemy hands and into the Allies' at the earliest possible moment.

To make sure of this, another change of plan was needed. It was with a considerable degree of justice that Rear Admiral P.H. Troubridge, commanding the easternmost of the British assault forces, wrote afterwards: 'If planning for "Torch" was horrible, that for "Husky" was hellish.'

A Massive Beachhead

At length the definite plan was adopted; this called for the 8th Army to land side by side with Patton's US 7th Army, north and west of Cape Passero. The beaches ran from just south of Syracuse on to the east coast of Sicily, down to Cape Passero (British Sector) then west of Cape Passero (Canadians and Royal Marine Commandos) to the American beaches as far as the tiny port of

Licata. The total length of the combined beaches was about eighty-five miles.

After the beaches had been secured the 8th Army was to head due north up the east coast to Messina, about ninety miles away, while the Americans were to cut across the island in a north-westerly direction to Palermo, about eighty miles from Licata. This division of work had been decided by Alexander and has been mildly criticized by the Americans ever since. According to them the British were selected for the most important task – the capture of Messina – because Alexander knew the 8th Army from the desert and was sure that it would be successful, while he gave the Americans, newer to the war, the less important task of the dash across the island to Palermo.

The Americans point out that their advance on Palermo and subsequent operations were so successful that they were able to secure Palermo, turn eastwards along the north coast of the island and take Messina, 120 miles further on, before the British, coming up the shorter southern route, were able to do so. This was true but most of the opposition to the Americans was provided by Italian troops, while the Germans themselves protected Messina. The US Army was additionally handicapped because it would take them a good deal longer to gain their port at Palermo than it would take the British to reach their first port, Syracuse, just outside their northern beachhead. At the same time the American beaches on the open Mediterranean were more exposed to the weather than were the British round the corner and partly protected by the land.

In the end, despite all difficulties, the plan worked well, but there were to be some anxious moments.

With the island of Pantelleria in Allied hands, together with the smaller island of Lampedusa, the invasion now had to wait for the last of its landing craft to arrive from America and the United Kingdom. These finally reached the Mediterranean in time for advantage to be taken of the favourable July moon, which it will be

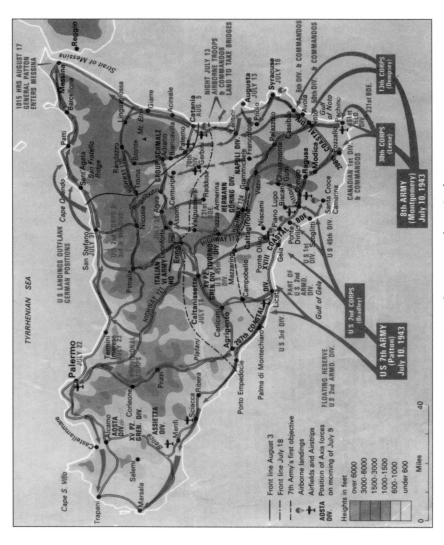

Map 2 – Seaborne assault on Sicily.

recalled had been the original target date of the planners back at Casablanca. What was required of the moon was that it should first light the landing of the airborne troops and then set to permit the landing craft to approach in darkness. For these reasons the date and time of the seaborne assault was fixed for 10 July at 02.45 hrs.

The whole armada numbered 2,500 ships and landing craft, carrying 160,000 troops, 14,000 vehicles, 600 tanks, and 1,800 guns, with the support of 750 warships and under an air umbrella of more than 4,000 aircraft.

Once this great force was at sea, or in the air, it was at the mercy of the weather. Earlier, on 25 June, Cunningham had warned:

> The soldiers seem to think that they will be landed at the exact spot they expect to be, and the weather will be necessarily perfect. The weather does not appear to be settling down, as it ought to be at this time of the year. We have just had four days blow in the Malta Channel, which would have made any operation impossible. The thought of having at short notice to turn back and delay all these ships and landing craft is a bit hair-raising. However, we have plans for it, and we reckon up to 24 hours before 'H' hour it can be done without much confusion.

A Sudden Threatening Storm

But 24 hours warning was not to be given. Only after most of the invasion force was at sea and about twelve hours from the enemy coast did a storm get up and then threaten total disaster – by the afternoon of 9 July a north-westerly wind was gusting up to Force 7.

The smaller landing craft rode up and down the waves like a giant switchback, one moment disappearing from sight altogether in the trough of the sea, then being flung high on the wave crests so that daylight could be seen under their flat bottoms. The larger ships, straining every effort to keep to the timetable, punched their way through the storm. Below decks the troops suffered from seasickness, the wet, and the heat generated by scores of men crowded in the unventilated holds.

Back at his headquarters, a tunnel underneath the moat which surrounds Valetta, where all hands were plagued by sandflies, Cunningham waited. He had already made up his mind that noon on 9 July was the last moment at which it would have been possible to cancel the attack. After that, he decided that there was nothing more that could be done. The storm might become so very bad that the smallest of the landing craft might be sunk, while the formations of the convoys of bigger ships were disorganized, but an attempt to recall the force at this moment would certainly ruin the operation, for it would be almost impossible to get all the signals of recall through to the ships. Some would go on while others turned back.

However, Cunningham, Bertram Ramsey, and others with long years of experience of Mediterranean weather knew that gales like that which they were then experiencing could quickly subside around sunrise or sunset, and this was what happened – about an hour before midnight, just as the assault force began to get within radar hail of the enemy coast.

An officer on an American warship described what had occurred over the loudspeaker system to members of the crew.

> Suddenly a little while ago, the miracle occurred. No matter where you may be stationed, you must have felt it. The wind died down almost as abruptly as it had started. Look over the sides now in the faint light left by a storm-clouded quarter moon which is nearing the horizon and you will find the Mediterranean still choppy, still tossed by a heavy surf, but compared to what it was only a short time back as quiet as if God had put His hand on it. This ought to be the best of all good omens!

The storm made the Allied forces an hour late at their rendezvous for the landing but it had also convinced the Italians that under such conditions a landing would be impossible. Cunningham commented afterwards: 'The Italian sailors apparently confined their small craft to harbour and themselves to bed.' Apparently they considered that on that night, at any rate, the enemy could not come, but, continued Cunningham in his official despatch, they came.

The convoys from Egypt and Tunisia and Algeria, from Britain, the United States, and the Canal zone, troopships and escorts with their attendant landing craft to which the men would be transferred on the last stage of the journey to the shore, headed in towards the coast. It was very tense and very, very quiet. The only noises in the component parts of the great fleet were the sound of waves, the straining of a hull and engines, and an occasional faint bell from someone's engine-room telegraph.

It was all going to be a famous victory, but nobody knew that then. Nobody knew what the opposition was going to be like, nobody knew how the invasion ships or small craft would be able to make their landfall. Anybody on board might be able to make a mistake that could ruin the whole operation.

Before nightfall on 9 July, the enemy had begun to receive reports of the Allied fleet and at 18.40 hrs on that evening all German troops in Sicily were stood to.

The convoys steered in towards the coast to pick up the submarines which were lying close to shore to enable them to fix their positions exactly, anti-clockwise from east round to north, they were *Safari*, *Shakespeare*, *Seraph*, *Unrivalled*, *Unison*, *Unseen*, and *Unruffled*. Six other British submarines and two Polish ones were off the Straits of Messina, to the north and in the Gulf of Taranto to help protect the landings if the Italian surface ships were to come out.

Enemy Astonishment and Disbelief
Shore radar stations were manned but their crews refused to

believe what they saw on their screens, so huge did the concentration of enemy ships appear, and they did not report until dawn when they saw, at first light, that one third of the entire coast of Sicily was lined with enemy ships, landing troops, tanks, lorries, guns and stores.

By that time, the first forces due to land on the beaches were ashore. It had been a mixed-up business in the starlight. Landing craft and boats lost their way inshore and ended up on the wrong beaches. It was discovered that parallel to the shore, there was a false beach, a hidden sandbank on which the bigger landing craft ran aground, so it took a little time for this to be surveyed and gaps discovered in it. Meanwhile, close inshore waves dashed the landing craft ashore so heartily that they could not be refloated. Altogether, 200 landing craft were pounded out of action on the beaches and £2,000,000 in cash had been lost in the surf – to be discovered later on.

Much of this confusion can be easily understood, for not only had there been little opportunity to practice this type of operation, but in addition, six months before 'Husky' took place, a high proportion of the officers and enlisted men of the US Navy taking part had never seen the sea.

Soaking wet, the troops struggled ashore; a few minutes before they had been seasick and apparently on the verge of drowning. Now they were quite suddenly ashore, moving with speed and determination up the beach to do the job for which they had been trained, for which they had come to Sicily. As they left the beaches, and began to move through the olive trees and across the wide plains beyond, there was, at first, little or no resistance. One party of Americans, accompanied by a War Correspondent, approached with due precaution an Italian pillbox, only to find it deserted. As he took stock of the situation a phone within the pillbox rang. The War Correspondent, who had been stationed in Rome before the War, answered the call with the standard 'Pronto'. The voice at the

SICILY – THE ASSAULT

other end announced itself as speaking from the local Italian headquarters and asked for information as to the whereabouts of the American invaders. 'Not here,' said the correspondent, 'everything is quiet here.' Headquarters rang off and presumably went to sleep.

CHAPTER X

Sicily – The Landing

It had been decided as early as January that after the clearing of North Africa the next step would be the invasion of Sicily. This operation was to be given the code name 'Husky'. The initial assault involved 160,000 men in nearly 3,000 ships and landing craft, starting from the United Kingdom, America and bases in the Mediterranean. The overall plan was for General Montgomery's 8th Army to attack the south-east corner of the island between Syracuse and Pozzallo whilst the US 7th Army on the left assaulted in the Gulf of Gela fifty miles away. The 8th Army was then to move northwards, securing the ports of Syracuse, Augusta, and Catania and the all-important airfields round Gerbini, whilst the Americans cleared the western half of the country. The enemy at the start consisted of two German armoured divisions dispersed in battle groups facing the area of the British landings, five Italian field divisions and six Italian coastal divisions. The fighting value of the Italians was open to question. Opposite the 8th Army, 206th Coastal Division was spread over about sixty miles, was poorly equipped and of low morale. The beach defences were continuous but not very strong. Inland the island is mountainous and movement off the roads and tracks is seldom possible: the domination of communication centres was therefore of primary importance.

General Montgomery's plan was for XIII Corps (Lieutenant General M.C. Dempsey) on the right to assault immediately south of Syracuse and for XXX Corps (Lieutenant General Sir Oliver

Leese) to land in the extreme south-east and capture the Pachino airfield. 5th Division (Major General H.P.M. Berney-Ficklin), stationed in the Middle East, was to form the right flank of XIII Corps and to assault on a two-brigade front, with 50th Division on a one-brigade front on its left. The right brigade of 5th Division (17 Brigade) was to capture the small town of Cassibile, nine miles south-west of Syracuse, and then move on to that port, whilst 15 Brigade (Brigadier G.S. Rawstorne) on the left, after securing the beaches and taking over Cassibile, was to occupy the plateau some four miles north-west of that place. The leading units of 15 Brigade, 1st York & Lancasters on the right and the 1st KOYLI on the left, were to land at 2.45 a.m. on 10 July, followed later by the 1st Green Howards in reserve. 1st Air Landing Brigade was to drop west of Syracuse about four hours earlier, and Commando troops were to land at Capo Murro di Porco on the right of and at the same time as the 5th Division and capture the coast battery there. 13 Brigade was in divisional reserve.

We set sail on the *Reina del Pacifico* from Port Said on the Suez Canal on 5 July 1943. Once out to sea, the whole grand plan was unfolded for every one of us to see. Every single man was instructed in detail on maps, air photos and actual models of the beaches. We learned that we were a part of a great army which was going to carry out a number of landings on the south-south-east and east of Sicily. Our particular landing was to be in the area of Avola, just south of Syracuse, with the object of taking that port. This was very important because Syracuse was, in fact, our main base for some time.

We were in 15 Brigade of the 5th Division, and wore the Y sign for Yorkshire until we joined the 8th Army for the invasion of Sicily, and then we wore the Desert Rat sign.

We rehearsed the order for departure from the liner, the various companies winding along each corridor, and down to the level of the sea, where there was a hatch for us to leave and jump onto the

British troops landed unopposed in Sicily.

*The Americans also landed easily,
but met the first Axis counter-attacks.*

landing craft, which would come along side. We sailed along towards Sicily, with not a sign of hostile aircraft or submarines – it was uncanny. On the 9th a gale sprang up, making the passage very rough and difficult, and causing much seasickness. It subsided later and left a heavy swell, but the weather had one great advantage in that it caused the enemy to relax his vigilance and enable us to gain complete tactical surprise.

At about midnight on 9/10 July, the liner hove to a few miles offshore, and we trans-shipped into assault landing craft. Zero hour was 2.45 a.m. The sea was still pretty rough, and it was not easy judging the time to jump onto the landing craft as it rose up and down by the side of the liner, especially being weighed down with full battle equipment. I had acquired a rifle as I was aware that officers were targeted by the Germans, who knew that we normally carried a revolver and ammunition, so this was a precaution. As well as my ammunition for this and my revolver, I had a number of grenades, gas mask, haversack with emergency rations – altogether quite a weight. As we left the liner, this was the only time that I felt the drama, wondering what was ahead of us, and when we were going to be fired upon. I suppose it took about an hour to get to the shore, and as we got nearer, we heard aircraft overhead, then the outline of the coast appeared, and we could see tremendous flashes near the coast and inland, as navel guns and aircraft pounded the area.

The Air Landing Brigade suffered severely, many gliders falling into the sea short of their target, with men clinging to them shouting for help, but we had to bypass them and continue to our beachhead. Our coxswain shouted he would pick them up on the way back, but he found navigation difficult; indeed, with a few exceptions, no troops landed on their correct beaches. Luckily opposition was slight and the results were therefore not disastrous. We landed some three miles west of the selected beach at about 5 a.m. but fortunately there was no opposition at this stage. I was first off the landing craft, up to my waist in the sea, and waded to the beach and the first bit of undergrowth, followed by the rest of the company. After we had regrouped, we proceeded inland, and after about a quarter of an hour, met the first Italian opposition. As we landed I thought, This is it, if there is any opposition I will be the first to get the enemy fire. But the situation was amazing. It was just getting light, and here I was doubling across a small beach and into some woods, with my platoon spread out behind me. I suppose that danger did not enter into my mind as I was so preoccupied with my platoon and giving them instructions. We captured some Italian prisoners and I experienced some narrow escapes from enemy fire when, firstly, a machine-gun opened fire on me when I was behind a tree: the bark was falling on top of my helmet as the bullets hit the tree; and secondly, an Italian officer was shot by my corporal after he had thrown a grenade at me, but, fortunately, I was unhurt. I remember making my way through some olive trees when to my astonishment I came across an old man lying prostrate on a bench, dozing or pretending to be asleep, quite oblivious as to what was going on, or so I thought. I let him remain there and I expect he thought he would be safer in this position with all the activity around him! The Italian prisoners were very frightened, having been found in deep holes in the ground, but, after a short time, when our troops had given them some cigarettes, they calmed down.

We, the British 8th Army in the East, had, by the end of D-day won the first great prize of the campaign – the capture of Syracuse.

British and Canadian troops had been guided ashore east and west of Cape Passero by the folboats (collapsible canoes) of the Combined Operations and reconnaissance and pilotage parties setting off from the beacon submarines and followed by command units. Weather and false beaches interfered with the operation, nevertheless, says Admiral Morrison in his history: 'All assault troops were ashore by sunrise: the cheery British signal, "Success" was made from every beach at 5.30 a.m.'

44

By 11 July General Eisenhower, in supreme command of all Allied forces in the Western and Central Mediterranean, could already send this message, which was passed on for all of us to read:

> In this Sicilian operation the United States and Royal Navies have again proved that even while engaged in operations covering the Seven Seas they can plan and successfully execute vast and intricate movements in support of land operations, and can do this, despite obstacles of distance, weather and enemy opposition. In this theatre, the skill of the Allied naval commanders and staffs under the leadership of Admiral Cunningham and his principal lieutenants – the American Vice Admiral Hewitt and the British Admiral Bertram Ramsay – are reflected in the precise timing and perfect technique displayed on the beaches of Sicily, where there were landed hundreds of ships and boats whose ports of origin were scattered over half a world. Their comrades of the air and the ground forces unite in an enthusiastic and grateful 'Well Done'.

CHAPTER XI

The Advance up the East Coast

We arrived at the coastal road, and proceeded east along it, meeting up with the other companies in the battalion, none of whom landed on the right beach, but we regrouped and continued our advance. Unfortunately, we heard that the hospital ship, anchored off the coast, had been bombed by German aircraft, but we did not know whether it had been sunk. As we advanced we met with stiffer resistance when we were confronted with the Hermann Goering Parachute Division, and other German troops, as it appeared that the Italian troops had little or no desire to fight. A Spitfire crashed near us, and although the New Zealand pilot bailed out, he was too near the ground and was killed. We overcame a number of incidents, and during the next few days the 5th Division advanced northwards, so that by the evening of the 12th, 15 Brigade was concentrated in the area of Melilli (twelve miles north-west of Syracuse) which had been taken by the Green Howards. During the night 17 Brigade entered the port of Augusta. Orders for the next day were for the 50th Division, together with the 1st Parachute Brigade, 3rd Commando and 4 Armoured Brigade, to advance via Lentini, and capture the important harbour of Catania by the evening of the 14th. The only operational task allotted to 5th Division was to capture Villasmundo, five miles north-north-west of Melilli, in order to open the road to Lentini for 4 Armoured Brigade; this task was assigned to 15 Brigade.

On the morning of 13 July accordingly the brigade advanced with the York & Lancasters leading. Progress was slow owing to enemy opposition, and the advanced guard was eventually held up by heavy fire from where the road winds with many hairpin bends steeply down into the ravine of Cava Belluzza and from the high ground away to the left on the far side. The enemy was holding strong positions astride the road and extending along the northern cliff of the ravine (about two miles short of Villasmundo), and an attack on the left by the York and Lancasters had made no impression. It was therefore decided to put in the KOYLI. It was on this day, 13 July at about 5 p.m. we had our first major action, known in the battalion as 'The Battle of the Gorge' which cost us a total of 8 Officers and 88 Other Ranks killed or wounded.

After getting as much information as possible, it was decided that the battalion should try to work round the right flank by attacking the enemy in position along the gorge on a frontage of some twelve hundred yards east of the road. The attack was to be supported by the whole of the Divisional artillery, the mortars of our battalion and the York & Lancasters. Zero hour was fixed for 5 p.m. and the artillery covering fire was to be about twelve minutes earlier.

At zero hour the battalion advanced although the guns had not opened fire, and did not in fact do so until three quarters of an hour later, until then the Germans were able to fire at us in comparative comfort. It speaks volumes for the determination of all ranks that we made any progress before the artillery eventually came into action. I do not know to this day why we did not receive the artillery support on time, as, if we had, the enemy fire might not have been so intense. We might not have received so many casualties in the battalion if everything had gone to plan, but these things happen in time of war. As soon as we crossed the start line, we came under heavy shell, mortar and machine-gun fire from the top of the other side of Cava Belluzza, and it was from then that we received most of our casualties. There was not a great deal of cover, and it was a question of running as fast as one could over open fields to the next stone wall. I proceeded on the right of the road, but these stone walls hindered the advance of the tanks of the 3rd City of London Yeomanry who were making for Tentulla Farm on the dividing line between the two leading companies. Six of the eight tanks were knocked out within a few yards. I passed two tanks stationary in a field, with no sign of activity inside, and was uncertain whether to approach them and find out if the crews inside were alright, but decided it would be too risky, as I felt sure the Germans would have these tanks in their field of fire – I would be a sitting target for them. It was just as well, as shortly afterwards, as I was climbing over a wall, machine-gun fire opened up on me, with bullets hitting the wall all around me. I remained flat on the ground for some considerable minutes before I proceeded further. By this time I found that I had only two men with me, with the rest of the platoon scattered in various directions, so I told them to give me covering fire whilst I advanced towards the gorge.

I was joined by our Second in Command, Major McRiggs, and together we clambered up to where the Germans were holding a line of a wall rising eight or ten feet above the very edge of the cliff. We managed to throw grenades over it, but could not scale it, and had to withdraw from the slope, eventually rejoining my company. Although it was late afternoon, it was very hot, and I remember picking limes off the trees to quench my thirst. At about 7.45 p.m. the battalion was in a position on a line overlooking the ravine, and at 9.30 p.m. we crossed the ravine, only to discover the enemy positions unoccupied. The battalion then formed a bridgehead through which the rest of the brigade passed by at 2 a.m. on 14 July. Thus after the initial hold-up of 15 Brigade, it was the KOYLI who opened the road to Villasmundo. The dead, of which there were a number of my close officer friends, were buried in the cemetery at Syracuse. For the next few days the battalion remained in the area of Villasmundo.

In view of the enemy's resolute resistance, the Army Commander now modified his plan. The advance of 50th Division to Catania was halted and the 5th Division was ordered up on the left to capture high ground about Misterbianco, four miles west of Catania, during the night of 19/20 July, whilst the 51st Division was to advance on Paterno, six miles north-west of Misterbianco, and the 1st Canadian Division on the extreme left, was directed to Leonforte, thirty miles away from Catania. The main thrust was thus shifted from 50th Division to the three divisions on the left.

CHAPTER XII

Sicily – The Conquest

Once the initial Axis attempts to hurl the invaders into the sea had been foiled, General Alexander intended that the experienced 8th Army should make the thrust towards Messina, whilst the US 7th Army tied down the enemy on the flank. But the British were soon held by determined German resistance, and it was the Americans who galloped across the island to capture Palermo, and then on to win the unofficial race to Messina, completing the occupation of this first piece of Axis homeland to be invaded.

On paper the 15th Army Group did not appear to have a great preponderance of strength over those against whom it set out, at least on the ground, and the ground in Sicily decidedly favoured the defenders. Once the Allied armies had crossed the narrow coastal plain behind their landing beaches, they would find themselves in hilly country that led soon to the precipitous mountains of the Sicilian interior. Away from the coast the roads were few and poorly surfaced, with steep gradients and sharp curves, usually overlooked from adjacent heights, and ideal for ambush; moreover the friable nature of the rock gave plenty of scope for the well-known skill at mining and demolitions of the German and Italian engineers. In such conditions a few determined defenders could hold up vastly superior forces, and on 10 July the defenders in Sicily numbered some 230,000 Italians and 40,000 Germans.

The rugged terrain made deployment off the roads almost impossible for vehicles and stores had to be carried across country by men or pack animals; only on the plain of Catania, dominated by the giant bulk of Mt. Etna, could armour move with freedom, though there it was impeded by irrigation ditches. Control on the road network was therefore vital to the Allies. 'It was apparent,' wrote Lord Montgomery, 'that the campaign in Sicily was going to depend largely on the domination of main road and track centres and these invariably became our main objectives.' The towns and villages of the interior, which were the keys to these junctions, were usually built on hilltops for protection in earlier times from those twin scourges, the foreign invader and malarial mosquito; easily defensible, they were to cost the Allied armies some of their fiercest battles and heaviest casualties.

In their favour the Allies held two essential advantages – command of the sea, and local superiority in the air. The Italian fleet based on the Gulf of Genoa, was too far away and in too poor a condition to intervene effectively, and the German naval units in the area consisted only of two weak flotillas of E-boats and one of landing craft. The Italian Regia Aeronautica was in a deplorable state with its obsolete and inferior aircraft, while those of the German *Luftflotte 11* were no match in speed and armament for the Allied aircraft. In a series of air battles between mid-May and early July the Germans suffered heavy losses, and Goering did nothing to improve morale by sending an insulting message to his pilots, threatening to deprive them of their rank and post them as ground troops to the Eastern Front. Moreover, coordination between Germans and Italians in the air was extremely poor. With their domination of the air the Allies were able, once the invasion started, to disrupt the enemy's communications and to delay seriously the concentration of the German and Italian mobile divisions, which had been dispersed across the island to protect its long and vulnerable coastline. The defence of Sicily, therefore, was going to devolve upon the Axis forces on the ground.

More specifically, it was going to devolve upon the Germans, for the Italians were lamentably weak in equipment, training, efficiency and morale, much weaker than the Allied planners could foresee. The defence of Sicily was entrusted to the Italian VIth Army under General Alfredo Guzzoni, with Headquarters at Enna in the centre of the Island. Guzzoni, aged sixty-six, who had commanded the Italian expeditionary force to Albania in 1939, had been recalled from retirement to take over this command in May 1943; he had never been to Sicily before, or shown any interest in its military problems. His young and capable Chief-of-Staff Colonel Faldella, had no previous experience of Sicily either, and had never before served with Guzzoni.

The Italian VIth Army comprised two army corps (XII and XVI) with a total of four field and six coastal divisions, and two coastal brigades. The XII Corps, with the Aosta and Assietta field divisions, was deployed in the west of the island against a possible Allied attack on Palermo. The XVI Corps, with headquarters at Piazza Armerina, held the east; of its two field divisions, the Livorno was stationed between Caltagirone and Caltanissetta, and the Napoli in the Vizzini area, west of Syracuse. It was this corps that would receive the first impact of the Allied invasion. The 206th Coastal Division held the south-eastern sector of the coastline, where the British 8th Army would land; XVIII Coastal Brigade and further west, 207th Coastal Division, guarded the 'American' beaches in the Gulf of Gela and around Licata. Mobile or tactical groups, created from divisional elements and corps reserves, were deployed behind them, close to the beaches, in support.

These coastal formations were composed of second-line troops of very poor quality, who had never seen action and whose training and equipment were well below standard. Their role in Guzzoni's defensive plan was to absorb the initial shock of the Allied assault, while the field divisions, supported by the more mobile German units, concentrated for a counter-attack to throw the invaders back into the sea. But the four field divisions, although the best Italian troops on the Island, were none too good. The Aosta and Napoli Divisions, composed mostly of Sicilians, reflected the low morale of the civilian population; the Assietta Division was better, but all three were under strength and their artillery was antiquated. Only the Livorno Division under General Chirieleison (his name means 'Lord have Mercy') was at full strength and reasonably fit.

The two German Divisions – the 15th Panzer Grenadier and the Hermann Goering, both armoured – provided a marked contrast to the Italians. Both original formations had been destroyed in North Africa, but they had been reconstituted from reserves, were well trained and excellently equipped, and were ready for action by the end of June. For political reasons they were placed under the tactical control of Guzzoni, but Field Marshal Kesselring, the German C-in-C South, kept in touch with them through General Von Senger and Etterling, senior German liaison Officer at VIth Army HQ. German/Italian co-ordination on the ground was not much better than in the air, and in fact, Kesselring privately instructed the two divisional commanders to go into action against the Allies as soon as they knew the objective of the invasion fleet, without waiting for orders from the Italians.

The precise location of this objective, however, was not evident to the Axis command until the landing had begun. Guzzoni and Kesselring agreed that the south-eastern corner was the most likely area, but Kesselring, haunted by the simultaneous attack on Palermo, insisted on the transfer of the bulk of 15th Panzer Grenadier Division – the stronger of the two divisions – to the west. After much discussion the German armoured formations were finally disposed in four battle groups across the island – headquarters and the bulk of 15th Panzer Grenadier Division south-west of Palermo, but leaving a small group in the centre at Caltanissetta; headquarters and two thirds of the Hermann Goering Division at Caltagirone in the south-east; and a fourth group, consisting of one third of each division, north-west of Catania. When the landings came, Guzzoni's best reserves were thus widely dispersed, and the inadequate roads, together with the incessant Allied air attacks, prevented him from concentrating them for a decisive counter-attack, before the Allies had established their beachhead.

If the Germans had even been sure in advance that Sicily itself was the main target, they would, of course, have garrisoned it more strongly. But they thought it might be a feint for an attack on Sardinia, and the ingenious Allied deception plan led them also to believe the Allies contemplated a massive assault on the Peloponnese. Faced by these diverse threats, and with their military power seriously weakened by the North African and Stalingrad disasters, they could for the moment spare no more troops for Sicily. Even when they came to accept Sicily as the most likely objective they did not expect the Allies to invade before mid-July at the earliest. All these factors, coupled with the storm on the eve of D-Day, gave the Allies complete strategic and tactical surprise.

When the Combined Chiefs-of-Staff decided on the invasion of Sicily in January 1943 they had three objectives in mind – to clear the Mediterranean sea lanes, to divert Axis troops from Russia, and to put pressure on Italy (eliminating her from the War was then only a hope, not a specific objective). The planning problems for 'Husky' were a nightmare, and apart from the uncertainty about the numbers and types of assault craft available, it was not known until the end of the North African campaign, in mid-May, which divisions would emerge from it in sufficient strength and condition to be committed so soon afterwards to Sicily. There was, moreover, very little time to train them for amphibious operations and prepare them for the very different battleground of the Sicilian mountains.

The land forces for the invasion, incorporated in 15th Army

Group, were commanded by General Alexander, and consisted of the US 7th and British 8th Armies. The 8th Army was to land on the beaches of the Gulf of Noto, just south of Syracuse, and on both sides of the Pachino Peninsula, while Patten's army disembarked to their west on a front of seventy miles along the Gulf of Gela. Alexander made no firm plans for developing the campaign after the initial beachhead, preferring to get the two armies ashore first, but he expected the more experienced 8th Army to make the main thrust towards Catania and Messina, while the Americans protected its western flank and rear. Patton's army would be the shield in Alexander's left hand, Montgomery's army the sword in the right. Admiral Cunningham reported that the Americans were very sore about their secondary role; they had, moreover, a more difficult maintenance problem, dependent as they would be on beach supply and the two small ports of Gela and Licata. But Patton took the view that an order was an order and he would do his 'goddamndest to carry it out'.

'The seaborne assault,' wrote Lord Montgomery, 'was an outstanding success.' On the British 8th Army front, XXX Corps (General Leese) landed astride the Pachino peninsula. The 51st (Highland) Division assaulted the south-eastern tip and had secured the town of Pachino by early afternoon. The 1st Canadian Division, supported on its left by a Special Service Brigade of No. 40 and No. 41 Royal Marine Commandos, landed to the west and cleared Pachino airfield, which, although the Italians had ploughed it up, was made ready for emergency use by noon. The 231st Independent Brigade landed on the eastern shore of the peninsula with the task of protecting the Corps right flank; this unit, which had arrived from Malta, where it had survived the full siege, made contact during the morning with the British XIII Corps near Noto. By the evening British XXX Corps was in possession of the whole peninsula, having suffered negligible losses and taken 1,000 Italian POWs.

XIII Corps (General Dempsey) made slower progress at first owing to enemy shelling, but during the morning the British 50th Division, supported by a landing of No. 3 Commando on its right flank, captured Cassibile. During the day the Corps occupied the high ground inland dominating the coastal road and railway leading north to Syracuse. Meanwhile the 5th British Division advanced northwards and in the afternoon rescued the few survivors of the airborne troops who had captured the vital Ponte Grane viaduct the previous night and had held it intact against the incessant Italian counter-attacks. Crossing the viaduct, 5th Division pressed on to Syracuse and at dark captured the town undamaged – the first great prize of the campaign. And so by the end of 10 July the British 8th Army had secured its beachhead and all its initial objectives with a minimum of casualties, and without meeting any Axis counter-attacks or indeed any serious opposition by land, sea, or air.

The invasion had so far been a remarkable success. Everything would now depend on whether the Allies could withstand the inevitable Axis attempts to throw them back into the sea.

The causes of the success of the Sicilian invasion, apart from careful planning and the skilled execution of the plans, may be summarized as follows:

(1) In anticipation on an attempt on Sicily the Germans concentrated a force of between 250 and 300 fighter aeroplanes in the Catania area. Their long-range bombers and the Italian bombing aircraft were stationed at various airfields in Sicily, Southern Italy and Sardinia. If the German fighter aircraft could be destroyed or driven off the field or neutralized in some other way these long-range bombers would be useless. Prior to the landings American Fortresses flying from North Africa concentrated on the German fighter aeroplanes on their aerodromes, destroying many on the ground and driving most

of the remainder away to airfields in Southern Italy. This was a similar tactic to that employed by the Japanese prior to their invasion of the Philippines; but the Japanese massed attack on the American airfields was concentrated into one day and the invaders had the advantage of surprise as at Pearl Harbour. The bombing of the Sicilian aerodromes went on steadily for weeks before the actual landings.

(2) In the week immediately preceding the landings the Allied bombers were switched to the attack on Trapani, in the extreme west of Sicily. The enemy knew from his air reconnaissance and other intelligence reports that an invasion was impending. The concentration of shipping and landing craft in the North African harbours could not be concealed. The German/Italian Higher Command came to the conclusion that the invasion would be launched against the western tip of the island. They had some excuse, for this would entail the shortest sea passage for the bulk of the invaders of 190 miles from Tunis to Trapani. The surviving German fighters and most of the weak Italian air force were transferred accordingly to the aerodromes in the west of Sicily, one hundred miles away from the main landing beaches. When the mistake was discovered they were too far away to intervene immediately, and by the time they had been transferred strong beachheads had been established.

(3) The landings were made on a front nearly 100 miles long. The defenders could not be in strength everywhere along such a front and the invaders reaped the full benefits of surprise and local superiority.

(4) Italian resistance was almost negligible and the southern and eastern shores chosen for the disembarkations were held by the Italian troops. The Germans were in the west and north.

(5) There was excellent teamwork and co-operation from the very beginning between the air force and the ground troops. The

fighter cover in particular was adequate. The aerodromes on Cape Bon were improved and added to and used by a very strong force of long-range fighters. Pantelleria and Malta served as bases for short-range fighters. Prior to the softening-up process by the Allied bombers working from North Africa the enemy had between 300 and 400 long-range bombers from his various airfields within range, but the survivors gave little trouble. Once the armies were ashore the tactical air force gave them full support and hampered the Germans concentrating for a counter-attack by bombing every hostile troop convoy on the roads. Thus on 11 July when the enemy command began moving troops southwards in earnest, 400 lorries loaded with Axis troops and stores were destroyed on the roads between Catania and Syracuse by American Lightnings and A36 fighter-bombers.

(6) Apart from the defeatism of the Italian troops, the general war weariness of officers and men alike, and political dissatisfaction with the Fascist regime, the Italian Army in Sicily was badly equipped. Many of their weapons were obsolete. The Italians themselves allege that members of the Fascist Government had a financial interest in the armament firms and would not agree to money being spent on new machinery for the production of up-to-date weapons. Better profits could be made by supplying obsolete weapons. Tanks and aircraft were for the most part out of date. It must be remembered in this connection that the Italians are excellent mechanics and in the past had produced some of the best aircraft, motor cars and warships of the period. In Sicily most of the Italian tanks were of the completely obsolete Fiat B3000 type designed in 1918. The type was unsuccessful then and was called 'the breakdown tank' because it usually broke down on the shortest journey. They also had a light tank, the R35, produced in 1935, which was quite useless in action. They had

practically no modern field guns and there was a shortage of the old types. The invaders discovered to their astonishment that a number of the coastal defence guns on the island were wooden dummies.

The non-resistance movement of the Italian troops could not be foreseen in advance, or if it was expected it could not be relied upon. As we have already seen, the Italian soldiers under General Messe had rallied and fought hard in the closing stages of the Tunisian campaign. It might have been reasonably anticipated that if called upon to fight the invaders on their own soil they would have responded. Certain of the Italian Divisions garrisoning the island had been recruited in Sicily.

The first troops actually ashore landed from the air from troop carriers and towed gliders. They performed service of the greatest value, particularly by holding positions inland from Syracuse and assisted substantially in the operation which led to the capture of this serviceable port practically undamaged. Six thousand men were engaged in the airborne operations. Under great difficulties, men of the first glider-borne force to be used in action fought magnificently during the night before the Allied landings. Although it was not possible for the force to fight together, units threw the countryside into night-long alarm. The principal objective, the road bridge to Syracuse, was taken initially by fourteen men who, with about seventy more, fought their way through in daylight and held it for fourteen hours. The force surrendered in the mid-afternoon when only about thirty soldiers were left unwounded or not killed, and their ammunition was exhausted. Another unit of the paratroops were charged by a squadron of Italian cavalry. The newest form of infantry routed this relic of a past age.

Though American warships covered the passage and landings of their own troops, Admiral Cunningham, later British First Sea Lord, was in supreme command. Immediately prior to the sailings of the great expedition he sent the following signal to all ships engaged in the operation:

> We are about to embark on the most momentous enterprise of the war, striking for the first time at the enemy on his own land.
>
> Success means the opening of the Second Front with all that it implies and the first move towards the rapid and decisive defeat of our enemies.
>
> Our object is clear and our primary duty is to place this vast expedition ashore in the minimum time and subsequently to maintain our military and air forces as they drive relentlessly forward into enemy territory.
>
> In the light of this duty great risks must be, and are to be, accepted. The safety of our ships and all distracting considerations are to be relegated to the second place or disregarded as the accomplishment of our primary duty may require.
>
> On every Commanding Officer, Officer and Rating rest the individual and personal duty of ensuring that no flinching in determination or failure of effort on his own part will hamper this great enterprise.
>
> I rest confident in the resolution, skill and endurance of you all to whom this momentous enterprise is entrusted.

Only hard fighting was now needed to complete the conquest. The battle for Catania was a long-drawn-out affair of tanks and infantry. The Germans had numerical superiority at the beginning, because the 5th and 50th Divisions, who finally beat them, could only be brought up and deployed gradually. The Germans also had the advantage of prepared defensive positions, which had been constructed in anticipation of an invasion. The plain south of Catania is intersected by a number of rivers, the most important of which are the Gorna-Lunga and its tributary, the Simento. Here the Germans offered stiff resistance, principally by the reconstituted 15th Panzer and Hermann Goering Divisions. The original Divisions had been dealt with in North Africa. Their successors were first-class troops, and fought a stubborn delaying action in

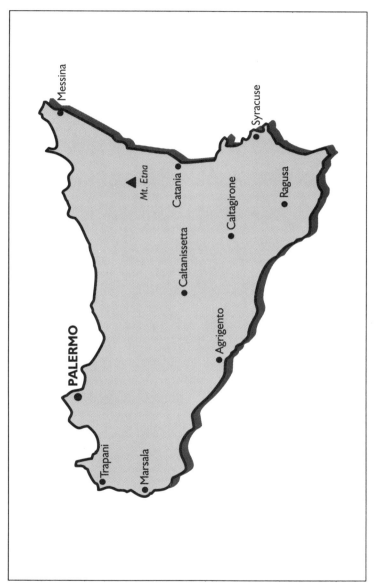

Map 3 – Sicily.

defence of Catania, Mount Etna, with its circular railway all round the foothills, and the approaches to Messina. Catania was not entered until 8.30 a.m. on 5 August, after I was captured. It was not until 17 August that Messina was entered by the Allies and all organized resistance ceased in Sicily.

CHAPTER XIII

Night Attack – POW Transport to Capua in Italy

By the evening of the 19th, 15 Brigade had reached the area of the Simento, with orders to lead the advance at 12.45 a.m. on the 20th, and secure the heights south of Misterbianco. The Brigade advanced accordingly, with the Green Howards on the right, the York & Lancasters on the left and the KOYLI in reserve, but it met with only limited success. At 3 p.m. it was decided that the battalion should advance on the left of the Green Howards and occupy in succession three positions which would bring the battalion onto the high ground two miles away to the north-west. We met resistance on the south bank of the river, and one of our carriers was blown up by a mine, the officer being fatally wounded. About a mile north of it the battalion took up a position under shell and mortar fire three hundred yards in the rear of the Green Howards, who had been held up at first light. The Commanding Officer appreciated the necessity of getting onto a dominant feature about a mile away to the left, and it was decided that the battalion, which had meanwhile assembled near a group of farms called Gardone, should attack at 10.30 p.m. At 9.30 p.m. the Commanding Officer was summoned to Brigade Headquarters and was told that zero hour had been postponed until 2.30 a.m. Meanwhile A, B and D Companies moved up to the start line, but for some unknown reason, D Company, which was my company, did not receive the new orders; two of our platoons were stopped in time, but, although the barrage did not come down, the Company Commander, myself and my platoon advanced as originally planned.

It was pitch dark, and I remember advancing across a field before we reached some undergrowth and trees at the foot of a hill. The last thing I expected was that in about twenty minutes I was to become a POW and was more concerned that I was likely to be hit by machine-gun fire and rifle fire which was all around me. However, my sergeant and a number of us managed to reach the wood unharmed and proceeded through it, throwing grenades and firing our weapons. After some time, it was apparent that we were being surrounded, as we heard German voices and could see them silhouetted against the background of the sky. Then a voice shouted, 'Get up, get up. Finish.' It was at this point that my sergeant said, 'I think we have had it, sir.' I said 'I think you are right, there is not much point in continuing, unless we want to get killed or wounded.' I shouted to the Germans that we would surrender and stood up to be unarmed and taken to their company headquarters, which was almost at the top of the wood. This was on the evening of 19/20 July, just ten days after landing in Sicily. I never saw my sergeant or men again as they were led off in a different direction to me.

I learnt, after the War, that Captain Hedley Verity, a company commander with the 1st Battalion, the Green Howards, on our right, was wounded on the same attack, and died in an Italian hospital later. He was the well-known England and Yorkshire cricketer and famous slow left-arm bowler. My Company Second in Command, Captain Oscar Scargill, was also killed in this attack.

When I was taken to their Company Headquarters, the German Hauptmann (Captain) spoke perfect English, and asked me the usual questions, such as my Regiment, was there an attack imminent, to which I replied, 'As you know I will only give you my number, name and rank.' From then on he said he was at

Birmingham University just before the War, and the usual remarks that we should not be fighting against one another, but together! His parting words, after I had been with him most of the night, were 'The War is over for you now.' I sometimes wonder what happened to him. I was joined by two other officers from other regiments who had also been captured during the night; at about dawn we were taken in open transport, similar to our 15cwt trucks, and escorted by two sentries, across the Straits of Messina to Italy.

We climbed up to the top of the hill, and found it was very interesting passing through the German lines in the truck which proceeded across numerous fields before we came to the coastal road. The Germans and their transport were all parked behind one another along the side of a hedge, and we certainly caused a great deal of interest. They nearly all had cameras, and took our pictures smiling at us! We passed through a number of small towns and in one town square the Italian civilians waved and smiled at us, and I thought to myself what a strange war this is, when your enemy greet you like this. I am sure we were the exception in this theatre of war, and elsewhere in Europe it would have been very different. It was a beautiful day, and the coastal route was magnificent, with lovely beaches and obviously holiday resorts, until we came to Messina. We embarked on a landing craft and travelled across the Straits of Messina; it was only then that I felt some fear and trepidation as we were wide open for bombing by our own aircraft, but it was an uneventful crossing. Continuing by truck we passed a considerable number of Italian troops resting on the side of the road, and then after about an hour, after passing through numerous small Italian towns, we arrived at our POW camp at Capua, north of Naples.

CHAPTER XIV

In the Bag

O n arrival at the camp we were handed over to the Italians and taken to the camp entrance where we were met by a British officer, to whom we gave the latest information about the War, then we were given a small quantity of food from their own Red Cross parcels, which they had saved for an emergency; it was a nice gesture and received with grateful thanks as we were hungry having only had some brown bread from the Germans, and a little fruit which the Italian civilians had given to us on our way there. All the officers there had been captured in North Africa, and were a fair cross-section of those who had gone into the bag from as far back as 1940, embracing all three fighting services, sailors, soldiers and airmen from Britain and various parts of the Commonwealth.

Anyone who had to subsist on either Italian or German basic prisoner-of-war rations alone for any length of time will know how dependent prisoners in both countries were for ultimate survival on Red Cross parcels of food. These took a long time to start arriving in camps in Italy, and the journey of the consignments from Switzerland to their intended destinations in Italy was hazardous – much more so than was the case with parcels sent to camps in Germany or German-occupied Poland. Of the consignments of parcels directed to German camps, with a signal sent to announce their despatch from Geneva, a remarkably high percentage arrived intact. The mere fact that it was *verboten* to pilfer was, by and large, sufficient to guarantee that pilfering would not take place. In Italy, on the other hand, stealing in wartime was regularly occurring and it was not in the national interest to be deterred by any orders discouraging the practice. The consequence was that the percentage of parcels which actually reached their destination was appreciably lower than in Germany. But fortunately, despite this inevitable pilfering, a reasonable proportion of Red Cross parcels eventually got through to camps in Italy. As soon as this began to happen in the summer of 1942, the prisoners of war, who had endured a cold and hungry winter, began to pick up considerably in health and morale. In some camps, with the arrival of parcels of food, and more particularly of cigarettes which soon became a form of currency within and without the camps, it was not long before a flourishing black market sprang up through any readily corruptible Italian guards, including a few officers. Most of this occurred before my capture, although I did experience a little of it over the next few weeks before we were moved to Germany. I was informed that in one camp, situated near a village in a rural area, local produce began to arrive in the camps, such as tomatoes, figs, and vegetables of various sorts. For the addition of a few cigarettes, the baskets of tomatoes, for example, would contain tomatoes on top as camouflage, while underneath were sizeable barrels of condensed milk, or butter and cheese. Thus from a state of great hunger, some prisoners now found themselves in a position of comparative plenty. However, the invasion of Sicily, and the war nearer the Italian mainland, caused much of this activity to be reduced, and any prisoner of war knows that the good times do not last for ever. Permission was obtained through the Senior British Officer from the Italian Camp Commandant for the prisoners to start a tin store, under lock and key, in which they could stack away some of the tins which they received in Red Cross parcels, as an insurance against future lean times, the return of which they all feared – should the thriving black market come to an end or the parcel delivery falter. This, of course, was what happened when I arrived, and it was fortunate for all of us that there was a reserve, and a welcome allocation to all of us for our journey north.

Air raid alerts were becoming increasingly frequent, in daylight by the new American Flying Fortresses and by night by the RAF, especially as their targets became the area of Naples.

CHAPTER XV

The Move from Capua to
Bologna in Northern Italy

I was at Capua from 21 July until early August, when the entire
camp was moved by train to Bologna and was added to a
conglomeration of other British and Commonwealth prisoners
from camps further south, such as Padula, which was in the
monastery south of Salerno, Sulmona and Chieti. The total was
somewhere around the thousand mark and the camp was virtually
brand new, having been built comparatively recently as barracks
for Italian troops – it was certainly more comfortable and hygienic
than most, with beds to sleep on in rows of bungalows. It was clear
to everyone that with the invasion of the mainland of Italy very
imminent, after the capture of Sicily, their own release was well in
the bounds of possibility. It seemed wisest to make some
preparations for an escape, should the need and the opportunity
arise. For many of us, the first priority was to make some escape
cake to take with us, to sustain us on any journey we might have to
make.

The composition of the 'cake', made from the nutritious Red
Cross parcels, took various forms, but usually the selected
ingredients included ground service biscuits or Quaker oats if
available – Scottish Red Cross parcels often contained this
nourishing food, which swelled in water or in the human stomach
and produced a satisfying feeling of repletion and strength. With
this were mixed such concentrates as butter, margarine, condensed

69

milk or dried milk from Canadian parcels called Klim and very rich sugar and cocoa. The result was extremely fortifying and dangerously tempting!

With the arrest of Mussolini on 25 July 1943, Marshal Badoglio had been appointed Head of the Government and excitement had arisen even higher amongst fellow prisoners. We had a radio hidden in the camp, and the news from the BBC was passed on to us by word of mouth by a representative from each hut appointed for this job. It seemed that the Italians had no longer any stomach for the War, which on 3 September reached their shores when British troops landed in Calabria in the toe of Italy. A collapse now seemed on the cards, but the camp routine continued and rations were maintained. Then, on what was to be a fateful day for us, all prisoners heard the news that Italy had signed an armistice with the Allies. The date was 8 September 1943. I learnt later, after the War, that during the night of 2/3 September, 13 and 17 Brigades of our 5th Division, and the 3rd Canadian Brigade, crossed the Straits of Messina in ideal weather over a smooth sea and without enemy interference. The assault was covered by a barrage of 600 guns sited in Sicily (an interesting feature in the history of seaborne landings) and by air and naval supporting fire. At 4.30 a.m. the leading troops landed on the beaches, which were not mined, opposition was of the slightest and the Italian coastal defenders, though equipped with forty-nine guns, soon surrendered. The Germans had already withdrawn. My battalion, the 1st KOYLI, sailed at 12.15 p.m. and disembarked at Gallico Marina an hour later.

The following was a report in the *Dewsbury District News* of July 1943, after I had sent my parents a Red Cross postcard stating that I was a POW, having been captured by the Hermann Goering Parachute Division in Sicily. At the time, the Commanding Officer of the battalion was Lt. Col. A.F. McRiggs (Raggs) who had taken over from Lt. Col. A.F.S. Douglas who had been wounded.

Staincliffe Lieutenant Safe

Lieutenant J.R.M. Newsome, son of Flight Lieutenant and Mrs T.H. Newsome of 'Longlands' Dewsbury, in a letter to his parents, which they received on Monday, states that he is well in an Italian Concentration Camp. He also says that he was captured along with a Sergeant and three men by the Germans. Lieutenant Newsome was reported missing in Sicily a fortnight ago and at the time his Commanding Officer wrote to his parents that he was last seen heading for a heavily fortified wood held by the enemy and that he (his commanding officer) had recommended him for the Military Cross.

Born at Edinburgh, Lieutenant Newsome was educated at Charterhouse. He was formerly employed by the Spen Valley Brewery Co. He joined the R.A.F. in 1939 and was later discharged with the rank of Acting Pilot Officer. He then joined an Infantry Regiment and gained a Commission. He went abroad in 1942 and served in India, Persia, Iraq, Egypt and with the 8th. Army in Sicily.

CHAPTER XVI

Italian Armistice – Escape from the Camp and Recapture

The day of 8 September dawned brightly as ever in that hot Italian summer, and at once rumours began to circulate. The first and most probable was that the Italians were pulling out of the War. Another had it that the Allies had landed on the Adriatic coast at Rimini, which was a mere sixty miles south-east of Bologna. A third was that the Royal Navy had shelled the naval port of Livorno on the west coast, in preparation for a landing there. It really seemed that the prisoners' deliverance was at hand, and more quickly than we had dared hope. But why were we still being guarded by Italian sentries manning the perimeter? This tended to dampen our optimism. However in mid-afternoon it was noticed that the sentries around the perimeter were leaving their posts and were apparently not being replaced. It was not long before the Senior British Officer, a brigadier, was summoned to the office of the Italian Camp Commandant. The latter explained that the Italians had signed a separate armistice with the Allies and that therefore he was withdrawing his guards. He handed over the control of the prisoners to the brigadier, adding that as far as he knew, there were no Germans in the immediate vicinity of the camp.

The Senior British Officer returned to the prisoners' compound and called a meeting of the entire camp and addressed us. What he had to say to us came as a surprise to many, though there was no doubt as to its import. Fateful though his instructions proved to be, few of those of us present realized exactly whence or from whom they emanated.

The story behind these instructions was, in essence, as follows. General Montgomery had been chosen as the British force commander for the assault on the Italian mainland, which was to follow closely on the capture of Sicily. He had laid down several principals of warfare, among them a doctrine for prisoners of war in keeping with his liking for the orderly planning of his battles, and with his personal lack of enthusiasm for irregular operations outside his control. He insisted that instructions were to be sent to Allied prisoners on Italian soil that they were to stay put in their camps until the advancing Allied armies overran them. He was not alone in expecting the campaign to be brief, lasting probably only a matter of weeks.

Some time in June, it seems, he issued these instructions and did so via M19, the organization which was in contact with nearly all prisoner-of-war camps in Germany and Italy, by means of a code which some of the prisoners had been taught before capture, to use in their letters to and from home. In July and August 1943 almost every camp, both those for officers and those for other ranks, received unequivocal instructions that, in the event of an invasion of mainland Italy, prisoners of war were to remain in camp and await the arrival of liberating troops from the Allied armies. There was to be no attempt to break out of the camp or to carry out acts of sabotage on their own account. General Montgomery did not want his future supply lines interfered with by any freelance sabotage or bridge demolitions behind the enemy lines. Nor did he contemplate any arms drops by air to groups of prisoners on the loose.

No doubt a factor in the formulating of these stay-put, no breakout and no sabotage directions was the low rating of a mixed mass of prisoners' military capability, especially if they broke out of camp and roamed the countryside at large, in unorganized bodies living off the land. After all, some of them had been out of

73

circulation for some considerable time and were probably in poor physical shape; in any case they were unarmed and although each camp had its Senior British Officer in charge, they were not cohesively organized, it was felt. So they were told to stay put and be patient.

Whatever the reasoning behind them, the instructions were clear and the penalty for disobeying them was spelled out. Officers who took matters into their own hands and disobeyed could expect a court martial, it was explained. The brigadier added that he had arranged with the Italian Commandant that, should any news reach him of the impending arrival of any Germans to take over the camp, he would immediately inform the Senior British Officer, who would then order the sounding of an alarm on the bugle. The prisoners were advised to be ready for such an alarm and to be prepared to move at short notice.

I and other officers moved back to our quarters in twos and threes to discuss the implications of this dramatic turn of events. We gathered up most of our belongings, and supplies of escape food in the case of those who had managed to save some. Finally, as darkness fell, we lay on our beds wondering what the morrow, and indeed the night, might bring. The majority of us slept, or tried to sleep, with our clothes and boots on, ready to move at a moment's notice.

Our answer came at about 4 a.m., before dawn. The half-expected bugle call was sounded and we all grabbed our baggage – for most of us it was just a Red Cross parcel under our arm – rushed out from the huts and made for the compound gates, both at the front and the rear. These were open, and those that made for the main front entrance surged along the road that led out, between high barbed-wire fencing on either side, with the guards' quarters beside the main gates. The distance from the compound gates to the main gates was about a hundred yards.

As the mass of prisoners hurried along, with those in the lead reaching a point within thirty yards of the main gates, they were opened, but, to everybody's horror, in the dim light, there could be seen the huge form of a tank with its guns pointing straight towards the advancing prisoners, completely blocking the exit. To a man the front prisoners and many of those further back threw themselves to the ground, in the hope that the bullets would pass over them.

But no bullets came their way. There was a deathly silence instead. Gradually those who had not yet entered the funnel between the fences on either side of the main camp road began to melt away in the darkness. Whispers were passed forward that the rear camp gates were still open, and the prisoners began to creep back to the safety of the compound.

I rushed out by the rear gate, together with a hundred or more, which opened on to a road that ran down the side of the camp. As I was proceeding down this road with a friend, machine-gun fire suddenly opened up on us and the bullets whistled between us. We threw ourselves to the ground, then I dashed across towards an area of woodland. I suppose I crept along in the dark for about 500 yds, but noticed that the area was surrounded by Germans, so I had not much of a chance to get through. Under the circumstances, I gave myself up and was escorted back to the camp by the Germans. Some officers managed to get further into the wood, and reached a house on the far side, seeking shelter in various outbuildings. One officer even went down a well on a pulley, and another dived into a pile of compost and pulled some of it over him for concealment. However, this put an end to any more possibilities of escape, and, as dawn arrived, so did more German soldiers with fixed bayonets and grenades at the ready, searching the wood for any more in hiding. Nearly all the escapers were rounded up and led back in small groups inside the camp. It was reported that a few, possibly a dozen or so, had got clean away, including the man in the compost heap and the man down the well, who sat tight and called the bluff of a German who threatened to drop a grenade down the well. It was when I got back to the camp that I heard that one officer had been killed and two wounded, one of the wounded being my colleague who had his thumb shot off, so the bullets did whistle between us, and it had been a narrow escape for me!

So it was that the majority of us were left in the camp, suffering from the shock and frustrations of the events of the dawn of 9 September. Apart from the fact that we were now guarded by Germans, instead of the vanished Italians, and the fact that there were no longer any roll calls – presumably because the Germans did not have any reliable figures to guide them in their counting – life went on much as before. Rations continued to arrive and one particularly alert officer took advantage of this and managed to get out of the camp by clinging to the axle of the ration lorry. This gave a slight boost to the morale of the rest of us, which was naturally pretty low by now.

Others made contingency arrangements to hide, in the event of their being ordered to move out of the camp by the Germans. Some made rudimentary dugouts leading from some air-raid shelters. One dug himself a hole in the ground and placed a blackboard over it, with some mathematical equation written on it, to make it appear that it had been used purely for educational purposes. His enterprise was rewarded with an escape to Switzerland and a post in the Foreign Service after the War.

The mood of the camp was a mixture of frustration and fury at whoever had issued the now clearly idiotic order for us to stay put. We felt that at least we might have been allowed a run for our money. And yet there remained a gleam of hope that, as each day passed without our removal, so the possibility of the arrival of our own troops was perhaps increasing. But in reality this hope seemed wishful and slender.

The outlook, previously so rosy, was now unmistakably bleak.

CHAPTER XVII

House of Commons Question Time – shortly after the Italian Armistice

BRITISH PRISONERS OF WAR, ITALY

25. **Mr. Driberg** asked the Secretary of State for War how many British prisoners of war in Italy have been able to join the advancing Allied Forces; and whether he will request the Protecting Power to ascertain whether any further transfers of prisoners from Italy to Germany are now taking place?

33. **Captain Gammans** asked the Secretary of State for War whether he can make any statement with regard to the number of prisoners in Italy who have been removed to Germany and the numbers who have escaped or who have found their way to Switzerland?

41. **Major-General Sir Alfred Knox** asked the Secretary of State for War how many British prisoners have now reached Switzerland from Italy; whether their relations in this country have been notified without delay; and whether the Protecting Power of the International Red Cross is looking after them financially and otherwise?

The Secretary of State for War (Sir James Grigg): I would refer the hon. Members to the replies I gave to my hon. and gallant Friend the Member for Lewes (Rear-Admiral Beamish) on 26th October and to my hon. Friends the Members for Stockport (Wing-Commander Hulbert) and Plaistow (Mr. Thorne) on 12th October. I am, however, circulating in the OFFICIAL REPORT information which has been forwarded by the Protecting Power about the camps in Germany to which prisoners transferred from Italy have been sent. Arrangements are made by His Majesty's Minister and the Swiss Government for the accommodation, clothing, feeding and welfare of British prisoners who reach Switzerland and for advances of pay for them.

Mr. Driberg: Can the right hon. Gentleman further say whether there has been any speeding-up of communications between the Protecting Power and the War Office, which were at one time very slow?

Sir J. Grigg: If the hon. Member wishes to make that particular accusation, perhaps he will put down a Question, and I will answer it.

Captain Gammans: Are there any instances of our prisoners having been prevented by the Italian authorities from escaping after the Armistice terms had been signed?

Sir J. Grigg: I should require notice of that Question. The only case I have in mind at all in that connection is one to which the Minister of State referred in an answer a few days ago. If the hon. and gallant Member will put down a Question, I will try to get him the information.

Sir A. Knox: Have the relatives of those prisoners who have escaped into Switzerland been informed?

Sir J. Grigg: Yes, Sir.

Sir A. Knox: Can the right hon. Gentleman tell me the number?

Sir J. Grigg: As I have previously said, I would rather be excused from giving any information about the number who have escaped.

Major Petherick: Will the right hon. Gentleman bear in mind that it would be dangerous to give the figures of prisoners who have escaped across the frontier, as it would clearly tell the Germans how many they had to look for?

Sir J. Grigg: That is precisely the consideration which I had in mind.

Following is the information:

The Protecting Power reports that the Transit Camps in Germany being used for prisoners of war from Italy are Stalag VII A, Stalag XVIII A and Stalag XVIII C, from which officers are sent to Oflag XII B and Oflag V A, and other ranks to Stalag IV B, Stalag VIII A and Stalag VIII B. British officers, whom it has not yet been possible to accommodate in Oflags, owing to lack of space, are temporarily accommodated in these Stalags. All these camps will be visited by the Protecting Power during October and November.

BRITISH PRISONERS OF WAR

9. **Wing-Commander Hulbert** asked the Secretary of State for War whether he can make any statement in regard to British prisoners of war who succeed in escaping from Italy to Switzerland?

17. **Mr. Thorne** asked the Secretary of State for War how many British prisoners of war have been sent from Italy to Germany during the past 12 months?

The Secretary of State for War (Sir James Grigg): There has always been some movement to Germany of prisoners captured in North Africa and, more recently, in Sicily. In some cases it is known that they were held for a time in transit camps in Italy. 2,400 prisoners were transferred from Italian camps other than transit camps shortly before the fall of Mussolini. I referred to this transfer in a reply I gave to a number of hon. Members on 21st September. I said then that it was probable that since the Italian Armistice the Germans had transferred British prisoners from those parts of Italy which they have occupied. Some hundreds of names have recently been received of prisoners who have arrived in Germany and it seems clear that large numbers of such notifications will be received in due course. At the moment I do not know how many there will be. The next-of-kin will be informed as the names arrive.

A number of British prisoners of war have escaped from Italy to Switzerland and others have reached the Allied lines in the South. Next-of-kin of these prisoners are being informed as soon as names are received. Some prisoners may still be at large elsewhere in the country.

The Protecting Power is continuing to do what is possible to obtain information about our prisoners and to safeguard their interests.

Colonel Sir A. Lambert Ward: Can my right hon. Friend tell the House roughly how many British prisoners have reported to the British authorities either in Switzerland or Southern Italy?

Sir J. Grigg: I hope that the House will excuse me from giving that information. As this process is still going on, I think it is extremely important not to say anything which may interfere with the prospects of the final escape of those who are still at large.

27. **Major-General Sir Alfred Knox** asked the Secretary of State for War whether he can make inquiries, through the International Red Cross, as to what happens to parcels of books addressed to prisoners of war, as a soldier in Stalag XVIIIA, to whom several expensive books have been sent during the past two year, has received none of them?

Sir J. Grigg: Book parcels addressed to individual prisoners of war in Germany are despatched through postal channels to the camps in the same way as other individually addressed parcels. If my hon. and gallant Friend will forward me the particulars, such as the authors of the missing books, the names of the permit holders who despatched them and the dates when they were despatched, inquiries will be made through the Protecting Power.

CHAPTER XVIII

Train Journey to Austria and Germany

We remained in the camp for about a further three days, and then in the afternoon what we had dreaded began to happen. First a large number of Germans marched into the camp, we were all lined up in groups of thirty and it was not long before the reason for this became clear. The main gates were opened and in drove a large convoy of German lorries with canvas hoods covering the tops and sides, and with canvas flaps at the rear ends. One lorry drew up to each group and we were ordered to climb in, and remained standing squeezed close together. Soon the lorries drove off in file, escorted with outriders on either side of the long convoy, mounted on motorcycles and sidecars, with machine-guns at the ready. There was no point in attempting to jump from the rear end of the lorry in a desperate bid for freedom as the Germans would certainly have opened fire. The most sensible policy, under the circumstances, appeared to be to await developments without doing anything desperate at that stage, and anyway, the convoy was roaring along at a great speed, so any attempt to jump would have been suicidal.

We had to slow down through Modena, where the streets were lined with Italian civilians most of whom looked by no means hostile and started cheering as they realized that the lorries contained British prisoners of war. However, shortly afterwards the convoy of lorries turned sharply to the right into a railway goods yard. We knew now what was going to happen when we saw a long goods train drawn up on the track, and then each lorry stopped right next to a cattle truck, which was waiting to receive its cargo of physically buffeted and morally shaken prisoners. It was a dreaded transport train, ready and waiting for its cargo of prisoners, destined for Germany. Suddenly our worst fears were confirmed.

Now most of us were having our first sight of cattle trucks as a means of transport – a sight with which the majority of us were to become all too familiar. The trucks were marked in French: 'Chevaux 8 – Hommes 40' (Horses 8 – men 40) and were in regular use all over German-occupied Europe for transporting not only prisoners of war, slave labourers and train loads of Jews to the extermination camps, but also, it should be added, German troops on their way to the various battle fronts on which their armies had become committed. Unlike the other categories of travellers, the German troops were of course able to keep the door open, which enabled them to see out and allowed air and light to get in.

We were unceremoniously pushed and shouted at to get into the trucks, each lorry load of thirty officers, then the sliding door was shut, followed by the noise of a bolt on the outside being moved over into position. The entire manoeuvre, which had caught us by surprise, was completed very quickly from the time we arrived in the yard.

Now all was darkness and a little claustrophobic, but there was an aperture about a foot long and six inches high, and at least the flow of air and light made the truck less like the Black Hole of Calcutta. On this occasion we were lucky, as this was the only time we would travel with as few as thirty to a truck; for later moves the number would rise to forty, fifty, and more. Even so, in the heat of an Italian summer, which had not yet shown signs of abating, thirty to a truck proved quite enough, and it seemed that a hot and uncomfortable ordeal lay ahead.

For us there was nothing to do but try to settle down for the night as darkness fell. It had been a traumatic and exhausting day, and most of us were soon asleep. Before the light failed a certain amount of order had been established, so as to make the best and fairest allocation of space available. It was found that the best system was to have fifteen people on either side of the truck, with their heads towards the sides and their feet towards the centre.

The train remained stationary all night. At dawn we noticed through the grids that we were still in Modena station. When it grew light, much to our relief, the guards began opening the doors of the trucks, and in turn each truckload was allowed to descend to stretch and to attend to the calls of nature on the adjoining track. After each truckload had had its turn, we were ordered back inside, but this time the sliding doors remained open, which was a great improvement. We observed that at intervals along the train there were flat trucks with no superstructure on which were mounted machine-guns ready and loaded and manned, in readiness to fire on anyone who managed to jump from the train. Escape was clearly not going to be easy or encouraged.

At about 10 a.m. an engine arrived and took its place at the front of the train. We learnt from the jovial train driver who was tapping the truck wheels that our destination was definitely Innsbruck and that another engine would be added to the rear of the train when we left the Lombardy plains and started climbing up towards the Brenner Pass.

As we remained in the station, an Italian arrived with a basketful of fruit and began strolling along the train, offering his fruit for sale to the guards and also throwing to us an odd apple or two. It was an opportunity not to be missed by one of the prisoners who had already acquired some Italian-type civilian clothes; when the guard was not looking he joined the Italian and took the basket of fruit from him. He then continued with the same procedure, shouting 'pidgeon Italian' with the original fruit seller following behind him smiling and talking. I observed the German guards actually pushing both of them away from the trucks! He continued walking at a steady pace until he reached the end of the train, and kept walking until he reached Switzerland, it was later learned. This incident lifted the sagging spirits of the other prisoners.

About midday there were indications that the train was about to leave, we were all ordered into our trucks and once again the doors were slammed shut. So off we departed out of Modena goods yard on our journey north. It was uneventful as far as I was concerned in our truck as we were unable to make any attempt to escape, mainly because the floor was pretty solid and we had no instrument to force up the boards. However, in another truck, I learnt later, one of the prisoners had managed to obtain an iron bar which he had smuggled onto the truck, and during the journey a number of them took turns at bashing away at the floorboard. It was agreed that the time for leaving the train would not be until dark. The train proceeded northwards across the flat agricultural land of the Lombardy plain, which offered little cover to anyone who might manage to escape from the train. It was unlikely that the train would reach the frontier between Italy and Austria at the Brenner Pass till long after dark, which would suit those prisoners attempting to escape. The idea was for someone to let himself down through the hole, but, instead of dropping onto the track, to climb under the running board and reach up, if possible, to the bolt on the outside of the door and release it. Once the sliding door was unlocked, it could be opened from inside and prisoners would be able to jump off one after another as and when the train slowed down sufficiently and the landing looked safe. As we crawled across the Lombardy plain, the heat in the trucks became increasingly intense and this, coupled with the lack of fresh air, sapped the strength and resolve to escape of all but the most determined escapers. With no food or drink provided, prisoners had to rely on what we had managed to save for the journey, and nobody knew how long that journey was going to last. We stopped at Mantua when the doors of the trucks were opened to allow one man per truck to refill whatever water containers he could carry, and take them back to his thirsty companions. We continued on our journey and by the time we reached Verona it was almost dark, and there was a welcome coolness. As we were getting nearer and nearer to Germany this was the time for the prisoners to escape, and it seemed as if the Germans thought so too as the bursts of machine-gun fire and rifle shots became more frequent. It was at about this stage of the journey that prisoners started to escape from the truck, whenever the train slowed down, and by the time it had halted at Brenner on the Austrian side of the border, there were less than a dozen left in it. The train arrived at about 6 a.m. just as it was getting light, and the German guards began to count their prisoners, truck by truck.

To say they were staggered by what they found would be a mighty understatement. Daylight revealed to the unfortunate officer in charge of the train an alarming discrepancy between the numbers of prisoners who had started out, and the number who had been transported safely to the Austrian side of the border at Brenner. For not only had about twenty prisoners managed to escape from one truck (no reprisals were taken against those still left, despite initial threats to shoot us) but another truck was completely empty by the time it had arrived at Brenner.

This truck had contained thirty officers, mostly Australian, and they had been fortunate enough to be in one with a faulty bolt on the door, which they were able to slide along, enabling them to leap out at every opportunity. From this carriage the entire complement of thirty officers eventually disappeared.

It was learned later that, out of a total of some fifty officers who escaped from the train, more than half got clean away. Of these the majority reached Switzerland, but a few managed to work their way down Italy to reach the Allied armies. A few also hid up for longish periods and finally joined the Italian partisan groups which began to form in Northern Italy. A couple of South Africans made their way east to Yugoslavia. They and other unlucky ones who were also recaptured and taken to Germany were able to relay the story of the mass escapes from the train when they were united with the bulk of the prisoners in Germany.

CHAPTER XIX

Arrival at Fort Bismark

The comparatively short journey from Brenner to Innsbruck, about thirty miles, took nearly all day, and as we heard air-raid sirens and bombing in the distance, assumed it was for this reason. It was rather frightening to feel that we were trapped in these trucks, should our own aircraft decide to bomb us. It was dark by the time we arrived at Innsbruck station. Here at last we received our first German rations – a hunk of dark brown bread each, before continuing on a second night's journey, through Munich and on, via Freising to Mooseberg. We were taken to a large transit camp, a Stalag camp, where we remained for a few days, and in the meantime, the officers were sorted out into groups, our group containing about 300 South African, 250 British and the remainder Australian and New Zealand officers, all placed together in one compound, with about thirty other ranks, whose function was, eventually, when we arrived at a permanent camp, to cook and keep the camp clean, and do other jobs. According to the Geneva Convention officers were not allowed to go on working parties.

After about three days the whole of our compound was moved by train, in the usual cattle trucks, to a further temporary camp in Alsace Lorraine, not far from Strasbourg. This was a different kind of POW camp, named Fort Bismark, in that it was sited below the ground. The building was rectangular, with only one entrance, and the wall around the front was about 15 ft high. See plan.

We remained here for about a week, but managed to become active during this time, thinking of ways and means of escaping,

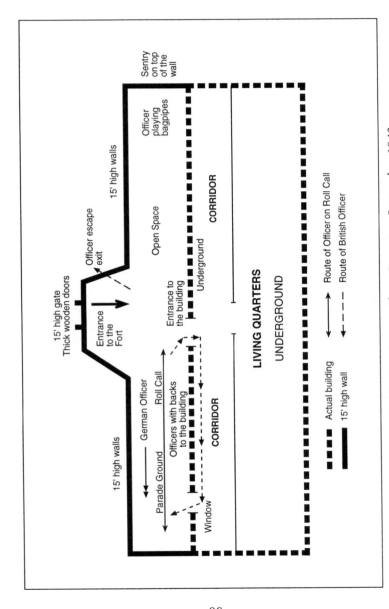

Fort Bismark, Nr. Strasbourg, Alsace Lorraine, September 1943.

and having various meetings to organize a plan. The usual roll calls took place each morning and evening, when we assembled in a long line of fours to enable the German officer to count us. One of the Scottish prisoners had managed to keep his bagpipes over his period of captivity, which he played to us from time to time, which was entertaining and relieved the monotony. One day he placed himself at one end of the camp, and commenced playing all the well-known Scottish songs, which most of us joined in, singing lustily. This, of course, attracted the attention of the guard, which was the object of the exercise. He looked down at us with amazement and must have wondered what on earth was going on, being fascinated by the noise coming from the pipes, let alone a crowd of officers singing in a loud fashion, not always in tune! In the meantime, whilst all this was going on, two officers were able to get into the recess at the entrance to the camp; one assisted his colleague to get on top of the wall by climbing onto his shoulders, and then he was able to heave himself onto the top and through the wire. This was accomplished at dusk, just before the roll call, so the next action was to ensure, at the roll call, that the figure for the total number of prisoners remained the same as the previous count in the morning. This was done in quite a simple way. The German officer walked along the front of the parade, counting in fours, and when he had reached the sixth row, one of the officers bent down and crept into the building behind, ran down the entire corridor, and got out of the window at the end to rejoin the last four on the parade, consequently the total number added up to the same figure as the morning roll call. We managed to keep this up for two days, until, unfortunately, the officer was recaptured and brought back to the fort. This incident did puzzle the Germans, and they threatened to stop the Red Cross parcels until we informed then how it was done. We were now getting a little frustrated, as the fort was not an ideal place to live in, with stone walls inside and damp, with no comfort, and us having to sleep on the floor.

CHAPTER XX

Permanent Camp – Oflag Va, Weinberg, Nr. Heilbronn

After about a week we were on the move again, about the end of September 1943, when we were marched down to the local station, and entrained on cattle trucks once more on a journey to what was to be our permanent camp for about two years. This was Oflag Va, situated at Weinberg, a small town near Heilbronn. It was a good camp with wooden huts, and each perimeter facing open countryside. We joined a few officers already there, and when we were all allocated to the six living accommodation huts, plus a hut for the other ranks, the total in the camp would have been in the region of 600. Each hut contained twelve rooms, with eight to a room, two-tier bunks and a stove in the middle of the room, which burnt coke or wood. There was also a wooden table, cupboard and some chairs. At last we felt that our travels were over for the time being, and that we could get organized and settle down. Our main concern was to enable our families to know of our whereabouts and address, as well as being anxious to receive mail from home. I had already sent a postcard from Italy through the Red Cross informing my parents of my captivity, so it was with relief that the Germans shortly issued us with a lettercard each (one a month) which was sent to our home through the Red Cross. We were also issued with a blanket.

My seven colleagues in my room were all in interesting professions: 1. A school teacher who could speak German, and was in charge of our hut on roll-call parades; 2. A director of a South of England brewery; 3. A jobber on the Stock Exchange; 4. An officer studying to be ordained; and three South African officers, two of whom were teachers and one studying to be a teacher. We all got on very well, but living together over this period in a small room, when the Germans locked us up from dusk to dawn, was a great strain on our relationships, so we did get on one another's nerves at times, especially during the winter months.

There were slit trenches outside each hut, and when the air-raid siren sounded the hut doors were opened by the sentries, but none of us used these trenches, even when the air raids became more frequent as the months went by. During the hours when we were locked in our huts at night-time, we spent the time reading, playing bridge, and many studied for professions with the books received from the Red Cross. We heated items from our parcels on the stove, and made tea or coffee. When the bell sounded for roll call twice a day at dusk and dawn, we all paraded in front of our huts, with the officer in charge of each hut in front. The Senior British Officer, Lt. Col. De Beer, brought the whole parade to attention, the German officer saluted him, then one of the German NCOs counted the officers from each hut. It was during this time that if any mail had arrived, after being sorted out into huts, it was then given out on parade by the officer in charge of the hut.

During the day, over the next many months, we were able to take exercise in the camp compound, and one usually walked up and down for an hour with a friend from the same hut, or we would arrange to meet friends from other huts. In the afternoon we would often have friends to our room for tea, which usually consisted of one biscuit and a cup of tea or coffee – it was a relief from the monotony, and an opportunity to discuss other matters of interest. As the majority were South African officers, as well as a few Australian and New Zealanders, it was pleasant to talk to them about their own countries, and later, as we got organized in

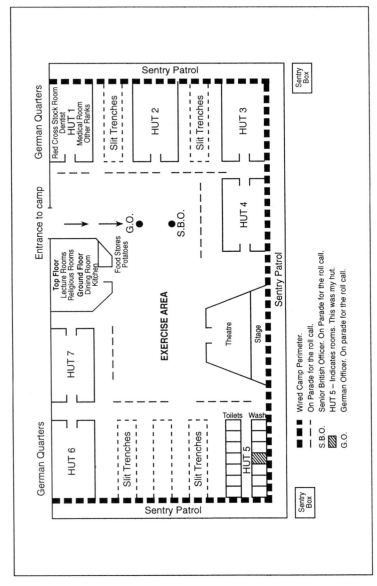

Oflag Va, Heilbronn, Nr. Weinsberg. September to May 1943–1945.

the camp, lectures were given from time to time, with illustrated maps, by the officers from those countries. It was very educational, and, apart from passing away the time, it served to create a very close relationship with our Commonwealth friends.

Within a month the Red Cross officials visited the camp, and a few weeks later, Red Cross parcels arrived, followed by medical supplies, clothing, books and other items. We came to rely on these additional amenities, as well as our mail from home. Arrangements could be made to pay for these items through the Red Cross and our bank in the United Kingdom. Although we had a basic weekly food allowance from the Italians and Germans under the Geneva Convention, it was only just enough to keep us above the starvation line, with a very small quantity of meat, 3 ozs of potato a day, sauerkraut and a little cheese, with twelve to a dark brown loaf of bread.

On the basis of an issue of one Red Cross parcel per man per week, in theory, the average parcel, together with camp rations, provided us with sufficient calories and essential nutriments.

Throughout my captivity, we rarely received a full British parcel per week from Switzerland, due to the rail damage from bombing. At best, half a parcel a week was the average, sometimes a quarter, or none at all towards the end of the War. A list is shown on the next page of the contents of a British Red Cross parcel; we always received type No. 1.

FOOD PARCELS

Commodity	Net Weight		Types					
Biscuits—								
Service Ration ..	8 oz. tin	1	2	3	4	5	–	7
Healthy Life, etc. ..	16 ,, ,,	–	–	–	–	–	6	–
Cheese	3¼ ,, ,,	1	2	3	4	5	6	–
Chocolate ..	4 ,, pkt.	1	2	3	4	5	6	7
Fish—								
Pilchards	8 ,, tin	–	–	3	4	5	–	–
,, ...	16 ,, ,,	–	–	–	–	–	–	7
Salmon	8 ,, ,,	1	2	–	–	–	6	–
Fruit, etc.—								
Creamed Rice ..	12 ,, ,,	–	–	–	4	–	–	–
Fruit, Dried ..	8 ,, pkt.	1	2	–	–	5	–	–
,, Tinned ..	8 ,, tin	–	–	–	–	–	–	7
Puddings, Assorted ..	12 ,, ,,	–	–	3	–	–	–	–
,, ,, ..	6 ,, ,,	–	–	–	–	–	6	–
Jam	12 ,, ,,	1	–	3	4	5	–	–
Syrup	8 ,, ,,	–	2	–	–	–	6	–
Butter	8 ,, ,,	1	–	3	–	5	–	–
Margarine ..	8 ,, ,,	–	2	–	4	–	6	7
Meat, Hot ..	16 ,, ,,	1	2	3	4	5	6	–
Meat, Cold—								
Beef Loaf ..	12 ,, ,,	–	2	3	–	–	6	–
Chopped Ham, etc. ..	12 ,, ,,	1	–	–	4	5	–	–
Sausages ..	8 ,, ,,	–	–	3	–	–	–	–
Bacon ..	8 ,, ,,	1	2	–	–	5	6	–
Milk, Condensed ..	14 ,, ,,	1	2	3	4	5	6	–
,, ,, (Vit. C.) ..		–	–	–	–	–	–	7*
Sugar ..	4 ,, bar	1	2	3	4	5	6	7*
Tea ..	2 ,, pkt.	1	2	3	4	5	6	7
Vegetables ..	10 ,, tin	1	2	–	4	5	–	–
Cocoa ..	4 ,, ,,	1	2	3	4	5	–	–
Mustard or Pepper ..	1 ,, ,,	–	2	–	–	–	–	–
Salt ..	1½ ,, cube	1	–	–	–	–	6	–
,, ..	2 ,, pkt.	–	–	–	–	–	–	7
Eggs, Dried ..	1½ ,, tin	–	2	3	4	5	6	7
Oatmeal ..	8 ,, ,,	–	–	–	–	–	6	–
Oats, Rolled ..	5 ,, ,,	1	2	–	4	5	–	–
Oatmeal Block ..	1¾ ,, block	–	–	–	4*	–	–	–
Pancake Batter ..	6½ ,, pkt.	–	–	3	–	–	–	–
Sweets ..	2 ,, ,,	–	–	–	–	–	6	–
Atta ..	16 ,, tin	–	–	–	–	–	–	7
Curry Powder ..	2 ,, ,,	–	–	–	–	–	–	7
Dhal ..	16 ,, ,,	–	–	–	–	–	–	7
Rice ..	16 ,, pkt.	–	–	–	–	–	–	7
Soap ..	2 ,, tab.	–	–	–	–	–	–	7

* 2 tins or packets.

Note—Type 7 is a parcel for Indian prisoners of war.

Contents of British Cross Parcels.

CHAPTER XXI

Contents of Red Cross Parcels

At some time in early 1940, the maximum cost per parcel, excluding packing, was fixed at 10s (50p today), but special parcels were packed for Christmas from 1940 to 1944, although the 10s limit was not adhered to. Other than Great Britain, Canada was the most substantial contributor of food parcels, which were very good and a nice change. We had an issue of 100 cigarettes or 4 ozs of tobacco a week.

In Oflag Va we had a central dining room where all the cooking items were taken out of the parcel by our own kitchen staff before we received them, and we were left with the jam or marmalade, margarine, tea, biscuits, sugar and soap for our own use, which we consumed in our huts, mainly in the evenings, whilst the dining room provided one hot meal a day at lunchtime. The potatoes were cooked and issued then, and some of us took them back to our huts to be eaten in the evenings. The Canadian parcels were different, namely, powdered milk, pilchards, corned beef, raisins, large biscuits and coffee. Each hut had a certain day when individuals collected their Red Cross parcels from the hut where all items were stocked. Our morale was continually boosted by the delivery of these items, particularly our mail from home; in fact we relied very much on the Red Cross, and I cannot speak more highly of them and their organization. We even had a swop shop where we could exchange items of food and cigarettes.

We received German newspapers each day and were able to follow the course of the War on the Western and Eastern Fronts on ordinarily careful. I have in front of me a long list of items catalogued at Oflag 64/Z—articles ranging from books to boots, from musical instruments to typewriters, food and clothing, all grouped with the utmost consideration and "bequeathed" to a dozen different camps where they might be of most use.

Replacement of *Padua* Parcels

The anxiety felt by next of kin at the loss of the S.S. *Padua*, which sank off Marseilles on October 27th with 11,000 Red Cross parcels, must have been considerably relieved by the War Minister's reassurance last month.

Owing to the reserve of food parcels established by the foresight of the British Red Cross at Geneva," said Sir James Grigg in the House of Commons on November 11th, "our prisoners will not suffer

His Xmas Dinner

Served from the following

Chocolate Biscuits	...	1 8	oz. pkt.
Cheese	... ...	1 3½	,, tin
Chocolate (Vitaminised)	1 4	,, pkt.
Salmon	... ...	1 8	,, tin
Bacon	... ...	1 8	,, ,,
Christmas Pudding	1 16	,, ,,
Syrup	... ...	1 8	,, ,,
Butter	... ...	1 8	,, ,,
Tournados or Rissoles	1 16	,, ,,
Steak & Kidney Pudding	1 16	,, ,,
Condensed Milk	1 14	,, ,,
Sugar	... ...	1 4	,, block
Tea	... ...	1 2	,, pkt.
Xmas Cake	...	1 16	,, tin

100 Cigarettes or 4 oz. Tobacco (packed separately).

Parcels of Sunlight

The home-coming prisoners have certainly been given a warm welcome. What is also most gratifying is the welcome they have given to us. In spite of the happy busy-ness of their return, numbers of them have found time to write a personal letter of thanks for such comfort as the Red Cross has been able to bring them during their time of captivity.

"For the first few months," writes one, typical of many, "everything looked black and the future held no hope. Then food, clothing, books, games and cigarettes began to come in from the Red Cross and the world became full of sunshine again."

Nothing Wasted

In the tumult and excitement of leaving camp our repatriated prisoners might well be forgiven if they had lightheartedly abandoned things they would no longer be needing. As a matter of fact they seem to have been extra-

in this respect. . . . Steps have already been taken to charter other tonnage for carrying parcels for prisoners of war between Lisbon and Marseilles. This will compensate for the loss of the *Padua*."

Food Parcels

The total number of food parcels now being packed each week in this country is 102,000, which includes 10,500 special parcels for Indian prisoners who do not eat meat. These are paid for by the Indian Red Cross Society, and are packed at India House and the British Red Cross Packing Centre at Southall. The above total, plus the parcels packed in Canada and New Zealand and the generous gifts from the Argentine, provides for all Dominion prisoners of war in Europe, and for an agreed proportion to Allied prisoners. It also allows a considerable surplus to meet certain contingencies.

Prize for an Essay

More than fifty prisoners of war entered for the essay competition, organised by the Royal Society of Arts. The subject was "Industrial Design," and the first prize of £20 was won by Capt. Rex King, of the New Zealand Expeditionary Force.

Pets' Progress

A letter to his mother, from a private at Stalag VIIIB, E.180, gives us news of his working party's pets. "It has been raining to-day and all our pets are inside, finding all the soft and warm spots. We are increasing in number and now have Scottie, the pup; Yantow, the kitten; Daisy, his mother, and not least the turkey."

Life in the Mine

Those whose husbands and sons are employed in German mines will be interested in the following comment I have been shown from a man in Stalag VIIIB. He works eight hours a day in a shaft "not deep—only 165 metres—and it's no worse than going down in a lift in the Underground. There is no gas in the mine so we are allowed to smoke. The lamps used are carbide. We wear leather hats and have a shower daily."

Believe it or Not !

Among those at Campo 52 were two brothers-in-law whose history in this war competes with the account of the "Two Brothers" we published last month. One "was captured at Mersa Matruh, the other at Tobruk, and they met first as prisoners in Benghazi." Parted again, they found themselves both at Campo 66; yet again, after intervals, at Campo 68 and 52 successively; and now—to cap it all—they have once more run into each other in Germany, in Stalag VIIIB. "We think this rather a coincidence," their wives tell me.

Proof Positive

In a group photograph we published a little while ago, a mother thought she could recognise the features of her son, so we sent her an enlargement to make sure. It was indeed her son—in fact, so we heard later, there was no doubt about it at all. For, while she was pondering it, who should walk in but the young man himself, repatriated from Germany. "It was quite unexpected," she tells me. "He looks quite well, thanks to Red Cross parcels."

Oflag Va, Weinnburg, Nr. Heilbronn, Germany. Sent home to Dewsbury by The Red Cross in 1944.

a huge map we had made in one of the rooms above the dining room. There were a Dental Room and Medical Room in Hut 1.

A committee was formed to organize theatre shows, which took place on the stage in the theatre during the day. Some excellent plays were produced; the acting was very good, whilst the scenery, considering we had little material, surpassed all expectations, which speaks well for the producer and his staff; an excellent job well done under difficult circumstances. We also formed our own orchestra. Baseball and basketball took place in the compound from time to time, and competitions were run between huts, which added further interest in the camp. Lectures also took place on numerous subjects; one of the most prominent lecturers was Angus Maude, a future Cabinet Minister, and Father Hugh Bishop, a padre in the Army, who became well known on radio and television after the War. Charles Upham, the New Zealander double VC, was another inmate in the camp.

CHAPTER XXII

Rev. Hugh Bishop

The Rev. Hugh Bishop and I became very friendly, and I helped to serve with him at the Communion Services in the camp throughout my captivity. He was an inspiration and guide to me over these many months. He became an Army Chaplain and served with the 8th Army in North Africa, but was captured at Tobruk in 1942. Whilst a POW he exercised a valuable pastoral ministry in the camp, sustaining many despondent men. After his release in 1945 he became Warden of the hostel for his community's students at Leeds University before returning to the Community of the Resurrection, Mirfield, as a Guardian of Novices in 1949, and was appointed Principal of the Theological College in 1956. He was elected Superior in 1965.

The Community of The Resurrection at Mirfield was only three miles from Dewsbury, where I lived with my grandfather and parents, so I arranged to visit Hugh after we were repatriated. I contacted him and he invited me to tea and to attend the service at 5 p.m. beforehand. On arrival I was taken to the library by one of the Brethren, who said that they were expecting me and would I wait a few minutes, and to switch on the lights in the room. I pressed the switch, and nothing happened, so pressed the second one and the lights came on, but within a few minutes a very bemused Brother came in and said, 'Welcome to the community, and kindly follow me to the Chapel for the service – Father Hugh Bishop will see you afterwards.' I said to the Brother, 'How did you know I was here?' Whereupon he laughingly said, 'We all knew

Rev. Hugh Bishop.

you were here because you switched on all the bells in the monastery, and only a stranger could have done that – they only ring for special occasions!' I kept in contact with Hugh here and at Leeds before he went to London.

He died, aged eighty-two, in October 1989 and was, for many years after the War, one of the Church of England's most distinguished and highly regarded priests who exerted considerable influence from his position as Father Superior of the Community of the Resurrection – the Anglican Church's leading religious order.

But in 1974 he created a sensation by appearing on a Sunday

television programme and informing an astonished audience that owing to his growing agnosticism, his disenchantment with monastic life, and his desire to share his own life with another person, he was resigning from the Community and becoming a secular priest.

The person with whom he was to share his life appeared alongside him in the programme and turned out to be one of his former pupils, Dr Robert Towler, who was by then teaching sociology at Leeds University.

The damage to Hugh's reputation caused by his decision and the manner of its communication to the wider world was immense. His many friends and colleagues in the Community were deeply hurt by the television appearance. He spent the rest of his life in retirement in London where he lived happily with his companion and celebrated Mass and heard confessions at St Paul's, Knightsbridge, and St Matthew's, Westminster.

What was not generally known at the time of the resignation was that Hugh had left the mother house at Mirfield some three months earlier when the then Archbishop of Canterbury, Michael Ramsey, who was the Community's Visitor, had informed the General Chapter of the Order that he no longer had confidence in Hugh Bishop as Superior.

The Community had, like many other religious orders, been going through a difficult time in the late 1960s and early 1970s, and, rightly or wrongly, some blamed Hugh for its instability.

Before this he had been widely admired as a retreat conductor, a strict but compassionate confessor, a fine teacher with a sharp mind, a loving and deeply holy man, who, during almost twenty years of responsibility for his Community's novices and theological students, had been a remarkable influence for many young men preparing for holy orders.

His increasingly liberal opinions – expressed in denunciation of American policy in Vietnam, of apartheid in South Africa and the

Smith regime in Rhodesia – were in no way at odds with the traditions of his Order, and even those who disagreed with him delighted in his wonderful sense of humour.

As a representative of the Religious Orders in the Church Assembly, then in the General Synod, he often spoke as a reformer on matters of current general concern. He was strongly in favour of a scheme for uniting the Church of England and the Methodist Church, and his visits to his Community's houses in Southern Africa turned him into a fierce opponent of all forms of racism.

When preaching in the Cathedral at Salisbury, Rhodesia, in 1966, a third of the congregation walked out, and he was subsequently barred from entry into Rhodesia, which kept him from visiting the Community's school at Penhalonga.

But all seemed to be forgiven, when on his eightieth birthday, the present Archbishop of Canterbury sent him a bouquet of roses. He is a man I shall remember with much affection. I sent him a card and letter for his eightieth birthday, and received a nice letter back from him.

6 EVELYN MANSIONS, CARLISLE PLACE, LONDON SW1P 1NH
Telephone: (01) 828 0564

28. 5. 87

My dear Jack,

What a marvellous memory you have, &
how extremely kind of you to write. Thank you very
much for your letter & card & good wishes.

I was 80 on 17th May — a Sunday. So I preached
at St. Paul's Knightsbridge in the morning & then we
had a splendid lunch party, organised by Bob
Towler, here when 70 people came to lunch. This
is such a large & beautiful flat that it wasn't
crowded.

I am so glad that you're well, & still working. I
hope work isn't too burdensome. I am so glad
you enjoy working in the garden — what better way
is there to relax?

I have plenty of happy memories of our days in
Oflag V A though I don't want to repeat them.

Keep well, dear Jack, & look in if you are
in London with any time to spare.

Yours ever

Hugh

102

CHAPTER XXIII

Camp Escape Activities

It is expected that POWs harass the enemy as much as possible, and always scheme to find ways and means of escaping. In the camp, an Escape Committee was formed, headed by the Senior British Officer, Lt. Col. De Beer; anyone who intended to try and escape had to inform this committee of the full plans. This had to be done and organized in an orderly manner, otherwise there would be risks and confusion, if attempts were made at the same time as other plans. Although we knew of many attempts to escape in the camp, they were never discussed in the huts, for obvious reasons, and we all learned about them on exercise walks. There was much activity in my hut when we knew in the room next door that tunnelling was going on. We had lookouts in the hut whilst the digging was going on, and empty Red Cross cardboard boxes were used to put the earth in and then spread over the roof as evenly as possible. The boxes were pulled through the tunnel by string attached to them, and a sharp pull by the digger indicated to the man at the other end to pull the box and then dispose of the earth. This was undetected for some weeks but, unfortunately, it was discovered by one of the three-monthly inspections by a body of civilians who used to visit the camp and search each hut. We were transferred to other huts whilst they filled in the hole, but when we returned the same procedure was adopted in another room, although no escape was made.

As the months went by we noticed that the bombing raids by day and night were becoming more frequent, whilst the sentries around the perimeter were giving us news on the progress of the War.

CHAPTER XXIV

Evacuation of Oflag Va – April 1945

With the advance of General Patton's troops in our area, it became apparent that our safety was at risk, and as the Germans were getting increasingly restless, a meeting was held with the German Commandant and our SBO (Senior British Officer), Lt. Col. De Beer (a South African, and a relative of the diamond family), when it was decided that we would all be moved by train within the next few days. Lt. Col. De Beer insisted that all the cattle trucks be prominently displayed with the Red Cross on the roof and the sides. This was agreed upon by the Germans, and, as we learned later, a necessary step for them too as the whole of their staff moved with us under the protection of the Red Cross flag. Their wives and families even came with us.

The day before we marched down to the local station some two miles from the camp, American fighters flew low overhead, dipping and wagging their wings in salute, then, in the afternoon, against the background of a perfectly blue sky, I saw a magnificent sight, something I shall never see again. This was 500 American Flying Fortress Bombers flying in perfect formation, with Lightning fighters weaving around between them, protecting them. I saw the silver tinsel dropped by the bombers to confuse the German radar, then the next thing was an almighty noise as the bombs dropped on the station nearby. We all thought 'That's it, no chance of moving now,' but the next day we were off and instead of forty to a cattle truck, it was forty-five, because some cattle trucks were destroyed!

The train only travelled at night to avoid the risk of being bombed during the day, and during this period we lay about in the fields near the railway track, whilst the train departed to a tunnel, remained there, and then returned to pick us up at dusk. It was the end of April, and fortunately the weather was fine and quite warm, but it was a strange feeling knowing that you were no longer really a prisoner. We were, in fact, free to escape into the country if we wanted to, as the Germans had lost interest in us, and were only concerned in getting out of the area as soon as possible. We were all relying on the safety and protection of the Red Cross, and no longer under guard. It was under this kind of situation that we continued on our journey, the train stopping from time to time, then we could hear machine-gun fire, but whether it was the Germans or the Americans we would never know. It was certainly very close and we wondered whether the railway line would be cut – we were all a little concerned. After about three days we arrived back in Mooseberg, which was the camp we had been taken to from Italy some eighteen months earlier.

We were allocated a small compound. The conditions were very poor, as the camp not only contained POWs from all countries, but many refugees from all over Europe. It was estimated that there must have been at least 50,000 in the camp. We had access to one tap of water for the 1,000 of us, but we knew it would only be a matter of days before we would be released, so this was something we could put up with. There were no sentries around the perimeter, and although we could have escaped, it was obviously better to stay where we were until the Americans arrived. I remember very clearly lighting a small fire in the corner of the compound to boil some water for a cup of tea, when I heard machine-gun fire very close to the camp. I took no notice and continued my task of boiling the water, which I thought, at the time, was more important, completely oblivious to the fact that there was a war going on around me! I felt no fear at the time.

We were then informed that a 'temporary ceasefire' had been

arranged between the Germans and the Americans and that a delegation consisting of the Senior British Officer, other representatives from the camp, the German Commandant, the local German commander of the troops in the area, together with senior Red Cross officials, were all to meet a few miles from the camp with the American commander in the area.

The American commander informed the German commander that he would postpone his attack for two hours, to enable the German troops to withdraw from the area of the camp to ensure the safety of all in it – an unusual arrangement in time of war! This was done, and some hours later the American tanks entered the front gates and were given a tremendous welcome. This was about three days before VE Day.

Within a few hours, we had the first good laugh for many a month when a mobile doughnut van was brought into the camp by the Americans, producing hundreds of doughnuts an hour for our free consumption! It was operated by two middle-aged ladies, whom I am sure have never been embraced so much! I have never tasted a better doughnut! Within twenty-four hours fresh bread was brought into the camp. General Patton visited us on the second day and was given a very warm reception.

It's over at last!

Nobody who was alive that day would ever forget it. It was a day of street parties and banquets and vast, euphoric crowds from New Zealand to New York. A day when couples embraced each other with joyous abandon in London parks and nobody minded. It was a day when the young Princess Elizabeth joined the crush outside Buckingham Palace and shouted herself hoarse along with her future subjects: "We want the King!"

For thousands, it was a day of longed-for reunions with loved ones who had been prisoners of the Germans for five years and more. The RAF had made it a priority to fly home PoWs, and on VE Day itself 200 Lancasters brought home 13,000 of them. Others had to wait many months to see the husbands and sons for whom they had prayed, and fathers they had never known. All over the world, oceans of tears were shed that day. Tears of joy for victory; tears of grief for those who had not lived to see it; but mostly tears of relief that the carnage was over, at least in Europe.

The prelude to all this rejoicing was a few days earlier. On Lüneburg Heath, a few miles from Hamburg on the road to Berlin, Field Marshal Bernard Montgomery, Commander-in-Chief of the 21st Army Group – more familiarly known as "Monty" – looked up with contempt at two German officers standing before him at his new HQ. "Who are you?" he asked an aide impatiently: "What do they want?"

It was May 3. Hitler had killed himself three days earlier and the Russians were fighting in the streets of Berlin. The Third Reich was in its death throes.

Monty's visitors were Grand-Admiral Hans Georg von Friedeburg, chief of the German Naval staff, and General Hans Kinzel, Chief of Staff of the German North West Army Command. They had come to open negotiations for the surrender of Nazi Germany, offering to give up three German armies facing the Russians on the Eastern Front.

Montgomery was having none of it. They could surrender to him only those forces facing the British – in Holland, north-west Germany and Denmark – not their armies facing the Russians. He strongly advised them to do so, or the Allies would blast them into submission with 10,000 bombers, day and night.

Next day they were back to sign a document surrendering unconditionally all the forces that faced Montgomery's.

The final collapse of the Third Reich came three days later, in Reims, where German general Alfred Jodl formally surrendered all German land, sea and air forces in Europe to the Allied Expeditionary Force and the Soviet High Command. The surrender was to come into force at midnight.

The European war – Adolf Hitler's war – was officially at an end. In the conquered lands of Germany and her allies, it was a day of disbelief – and for some, despair. And in almost every German home there was a tell-tale white patch on the wall where Hitler's portrait had hung not long before.

When the Reims surrender was signed, at 2.41am on May 7, In London, Britain's Prime Minister, Winston Churchill, was asleep. His Principal Private Secretary, John Martin, thought of waking him with the news but he knew that five years previously Churchill had given orders that he was to be woken up only if Britain was being invaded. He let him sleep on. It was left to Capt Richard Pim, in charge of Churchill's map room, to break the news of the surrender when the Prime Minister awoke on the morning of May 7. As Martin Gilbert reports in his book *The Day the War Ended* (reviewed on page 34), Churchill told him: "For five years you have brought me bad news, sometimes worse than others. Now you have redeemed yourself."

That day should have been VE Day. Churchill intended to broadcast the news of the surrender, getting the celebrations officially underway at 6pm. Instead, May 7 was a day of rumour and confusion.

Stalin sought to delay any announcement until another formal surrender could be made to his General Zhukov in Berlin. But word had got out.

> 'With a breaking voice, Churchill ended with the words: God save the King'

It was broadcast first by the German Foreign Minister, then by the BBC and the British evening newspapers. Expectant crowds gathered in central London and New York. A brass band started up in Piccadilly Circus and a bonfire was lit in Shaftesbury Avenue. Times Square, New York, was ankle-deep in ticker tape. Still no official announcement came.

By the next day, Churchill had decided that the people could wait no longer. In Britain, May 8 was declared a public holiday. At 3pm, 50 years ago tomorrow, Churchill broadcast the long-awaited news of victory. The "foul aggressor" had been defeated, he said, and the evil-doers lay prostrate before Britain and her Allies. With a breaking voice, he ended with these words: "Advance, Britannia! Long live the cause of freedom! God save the King."

It had seemed, five years earlier when Britain and her empire stood alone, that no power on earth could halt Hitler's *Blitzkrieg*, his "lightning war". But Britain never gave up. Her pilots won the battle for her skies. The German invasion, constantly expected, never came. And from D-Day – June 6, 1944 - onwards, the Allies closed in relentlessly from East and West, until that fateful encounter between Montgomery and the German officers on Lüneburg Heath.

Noël Coward noted in his diary for May 8: "I suppose this is the greatest day in our history."

It's over at last!

CHAPTER XXV

Repatriation and Victory Parade, London, June 1945

O n VE Day+1 we were moved by transport by the Americans to an emergency air landing strip in a field some two miles from the camp, and flown to Paris. A sad incident happened before I was airlifted from this field. Some thirty aircraft were parked on the side of the field, and, as one aircraft was taking off it skidded to the side on the wet ground, and smashed into a number of aircraft parked there, killing the pilot. Some of my friends were on the plane but managed to escape uninjured. On landing in Paris we were handed over to the RAF on VE Day+2, and were given a wonderful reception in one of the hangers, and our first good substantial meal for years. We were then flown out by the RAF to the United Kingdom, and my vivid experience on that day was kneeling behind the pilot as we flew over the White Cliffs of Dover, and thereon to Blackbush Aerodrome, near Aylesbury in Bucks. It was a very emotional feeling – Freedom At Last – with a wonderful reception at the airport, especially by the WAAF (never to be forgotten) – another good meal, refitted with new uniform, issued with double ration cards, and within two days we were sent home on six weeks' leave.

During my six weeks' leave, my friend, who had recently returned from Burma, and I attended the Victory Parade. We stayed at the Strand Palace Hotel and in order to get a good position on The Mall, we arrived there at 5 a.m. Even at this hour the route was packed, many people staying overnight in tents and blankets, and, as we moved around to get a good position, the atmosphere was terrific, with people singing, dancing, cooking breakfasts, and entertainers. We made our way up to the saluting base which was in the centre of The Mall, and placed ourselves opposite it, by entering and sitting on a specially constructed stand. We were first on at the time, sitting on about the sixth row, when, as it gradually filled up as the hours went by, to my astonishment, I observed an official asking people for their tickets! It was then that I learnt that we were in a special stand for VIPs and their wives employed by the BBC. I told my friend to sit tight and await the consequences, but much to our relief, the official stopped asking for tickets one row from us, consequently we had the best seat on the parade, exactly opposite all the dignitaries and their wives – something we never imagined, and never to be forgotten. I should mention that we were sitting amongst the camera crews who were filming the whole event! Afterwards we joined the crowd outside Buckingham Palace.

August 1945. The 1st Battalion KOYLI revisit the
scene of the Battle of Minden.

CHAPTER XXVI

Back to the First Battalion

In June 1945 I was posted to Ambergate Sub-District, Nr. Derby.
I had a staff job there for about two months until I received
instructions to report back to my battalion, the 1st Bn. The King's
Own Yorkshire Light Infantry, now stationed at Wolfentbuttel,
near Hanover, Germany. At the time I was somewhat disappointed
to leave Ambergate, as I had no desire to involve myself in infantry
training again, however, on arrival at Battalion Headquarters, I
was surprised and delighted to meet again my past Company
Commander, who was now the Commanding Officer of the
battalion. Nic Pope was a first-class regular officer, and had
commanded the battalion in Italy, and at our landing at Marseilles
in March 1945, before travelling through France to Belgium and
Germany. The battalion fought the last battle of the war at Potrau,
a small village some twenty-five miles SE of Hamburg.

We had a long and interesting discussion in private over the events
during the last two years, then I said to him, 'Why have you brought
me back to the battalion, as I have forgotten most of what I learnt?'
He replied, 'Just the job for you, Jumbo. I am putting you in charge
of the PRI (President of the Regimental Association) as I want you to
finish up in the Regiment.' That said it all for me, as I was proud of
the Regiment, which my grandfather served in when he was the
Chief Recruiting Officer for the West Riding of Yorkshire in the First
World War. Nic Pope was the only officer that I now knew with the
battalion since I left them in Sicily, as all the other officers had either
been killed, wounded or promoted and posted to other units.

110

OBITUARIES

We regret to report the deaths of the following members of the Regiment, and offer our sincere sympathy to their relatives:—

Colonel N. S. Pope, MBE, MC. Nic Pope died at Catterick Military Hospital on 9th July, 1983, aged 71. His funeral at Catterick was attended by many members of the Regiment.

He was educated at Charterhouse and RMC Sandhurst, and was gazetted into the KOYLI in 1932. His early service was with the 2nd Battalion in India and Burma, but he returned home to join the 1st Battalion and served with them through the '39-'45 War. Peter St. Clair-Ford writes:—

"Nic was a loyal Regimental Officer, and I particularly remember his success as Second-in-Command during the Italian Campaign. He was utterly fearless under all conditions, and was always on hand when wanted. Any successes the 1st Battalion KOYLI had in this Campaign were largely due to his sound administrative ability and his flair for improvisation. An outstanding Regimental Officer in every way."

He commanded the 1st Battalion in the final actions of the war at the crossing of the Elbe, and was awarded the DSO. After serving on the Staff in Malaya, and as an Instructor at the Amphibious Warfare School, he again took command of the 1st Battalion in 1952 for a memorable tour in Dortmund, Berlin and Kenya. Members of the Battalion then remember him with great affection as a splendidly idiosyncratic C.O. for whom the Battalion came first, and the rest nowhere: His command philosophy was well expressed when later,

teaching at the School of Infantry, he addressed a group of C.O.s designate as follows:—

"You are about to achieve that appointment towards which you have striven for many years. Be aware that one of your prime tasks will be to shelter your Battalion from the onslaughts of the outside world. If you suffer in the process, then this is a price you may have to pay. Above all, beware of unconsciously using your Battalion as a means of personal advancement or advertisement. It is one thing to be a " WILCO " Commanding Officer and another to agree to all orders and requests for motives which may be mixed."

He retired in 1962 and became a much loved and respected Regimental Secretary for 15 years. Bill Vickers writes:—

"I was sad to hear Nic Pope has left us. I knew him well and served on and off for some 30 years in the idyllic days of 2/KOYLI in Agra and Burma, next the dark days of 1940 after Norway, as his 2 I.C. in Berlin in the '60s and later in NATO at Fontainebleau.

Nic was a most able and successful Battalion Commander. I think I/KOYLI in Dortmund/Berlin were as efficient, happy and proud a Battalion as the Regiment has known. Nic was a real C.O. No one was ever in any doubt as to what he wanted. He set and demanded the highest standards.

He was a real athlete. Leslie Wieler used to say that Nic's style of sprinting was as near perfection as possible. His high hurdling was of International Class. Just to show his class he was a post entry in the All India 440 Low Hurdles in 1934. He had never run this race before. He won by yards. Twelve years later he won the Army 120 Hurdles in Aldershot as a Lt.-Colonel. He played all games imaginable with skill and enthusiasm. He was an accomplished sportsman, an exceptional fisherman and a fine shot.

My greatest memory of Nic will always be his interest in the younger generation. They flocked to him and sat at his feet listening. He taught them much and they adored him.

Nic was essentially a Regimental Soldier. He was a natural leader, proven in battle, and he had that rare and wonderful quality which made people really support him and work for him, not just 100% but that magical 110%.

We shall all miss Nic and his faithful service to KOYLI will never be forgotten."

He will indeed be sadly missed by the Regiment. We acknowledge with gratitude that he left his medals and a legacy to the Museum.

CHAPTER XXVII

Final Days in the Army

I spent a further happy period in the battalion with my own office in a large building at Wolfenbuttel, with a canteen and ballroom, and a staff of six, organizing the entertainment of the battalion, ENSA concerts, NAAFI supplies, civilian staff, canteen meals, and in charge of a very good dance band, which the battalion had acquired during the occupation of Germany. The band leader was a Czech, named Mario, a very pleasant man, who at one time was the owner of a dance band in Berlin, together with his delightful girlfriend, Swatjar, also a Czech. This was his own dance band, consisting of about twenty-four musicians – Poles and Czechs – including a few women. They entertained on the stage in the canteen and played in the ballroom on dance nights; needless to say, fraternizing with the Germans was taking place. They were all well looked after – their wages paid by my office – and all their meals in the canteen were free, which was a great luxury and for the civilians in those days when food was scarce. They were an exceptionally good band and I became friendly with Mario, who lent me his civilian car from time to time. I also employed quite a character, a Latvian, who was well in with the black market enabling us to obtain pigs and poultry for canteen meals, to which I closed a blind eye when I paid him.

Whilst at Wolfenbuttel I tried my hand at riding on the horses that the battalion had acquired in Germany. I had never ridden on a horse before, but three of my friends encouraged me and the sergeant in charge of the stables assured me that the horse I would ride was very docile. This proved to be the case and I enjoyed my first ride in the country. On the next occasion I was unable to have the same horse, but the sergeant assured me again that this horse was also very docile, and should be no problem to me – little did I know at the time! This was not to be the case, the horse knew I had no real control over him and 'took me for a ride'. My friends decided to canter over a field, so naturally my horse had to join them, much to my horror! Then a covey of partridge got up in the field, which caused the horse to rear, although I did just manage to stay on, then finally he kept slipping on the cobbled roads, which was the 'final straw'! Enough was enough, and although I never fell off, I was greatly relieved to dismount, and have never ridden since.

It was a pleasant way to terminate my Army service about a year later, after we had left Wolfenbuttel and the battalion moved to Bergedorf, Nr. Hamburg, when my Group 27 came up for demobilisation. I visited Hamburg from time to time, and will never forget the utter devastation of the town from the Allied bombing, although I was able to celebrate my birthday in March at the Atlantic Hotel in the town, which was only slightly damaged.

May 1946. Captain J.R.M. Newsome, Bad Oeynhausen, Germany.

My friend, Major David Lee, from Dewsbury, happened to have a Staff job at Army Headquarters, at Bad Oeynaussen, so was able to join the party. My last two nights in the Army were spent there before I left for the United Kingdom. The German people were generally sullen, which was natural at that time, but were co-operative and helped in the reconstruction. As I was constantly in touch with German civilians, I had a civilian interpreter to help me.

I was demobbed at Fulford, York, in May 1946, and have maintained contact with the Regiment and friends ever since.

The King's Own Yorkshire Light Infantry – July 1968 – The First Battalion

The Regiment was disbanded in 1969 into The Light Infantry Regiment, and we became the Second Battalion The Light Infantry.

The photograph (see next page) of the Battalion Staff shows Lt. Col. A.C. Elcomb as the last Commanding Officer. He is the brother of a subaltern friend of mine, Michael Elcomb, who was with me in the early part of the War up to the invasion of Sicily. Michael Elcomb signed on as a regular Officer, and eventually also became CO of the First Battalion. He has now retired and lives in Warminster with his wife.

The Battalion Staff.

The Battalion marching past, Allied Forces Day, Berlin 1968.

Regimental Headquarters – July 1968

On the left, Lt. Col. Nic Pope with his dog at Pontefract Barracks. Nic was my Company Commander in Persia, and was CO of the 1st. Battalion when I rejoined them in Wolfenbuttel, Nr. Hanover after I was repatriated in 1945. He retired from the Army in 1962 and became the regimental Secretary for fifteen years.

Regimental Headquarters. Back Row l-r: Pte E. Webb, W.O. II S. Brayshaw, Mr H. Holmes, Cpl. D. Bond. Front Row l-r: Col. N.S. Pope, Mrs J. Thompson, Mrs N. Nash, Capt. F.G. Young.

APPENDIX III

THE LIGHT INFANTRY

(13, 32, 46, 51, 53, 68, 85, 105 and 106)

A Bugle Horn, stringed, in Silver

The Sphinx superscribed Egypt. A Mural Crown superscribed Jellalabad.

Aucto Splendore Resurgo. Cede Nullis. Faithful.

BATTLE HONOURS

Gibraltar 1704-5, Dettingen, Minden, Nieuport, St Lucia 1796, Tournay, Dominica, **Corunna,** Rolica, Vimiera, Martinique 1809, Talavera, **Fuentes d'Onor, Salamanca, Vittoria, Pyrenees, Nivelle,** Nive, **Orthes,** Toulouse, **Peninsula, Bladensburg, Waterloo,** Ava, Aliwal, Sobraon, Ghuznee 1839, **Affghanistan 1839,** Cabool 1842, Mooltan, Goojerat, Punjaub, Alma, **Inkerman, Sevastopol,** Reshire, Bushire, Koosh-ab, **Persia, Lucknow, New Zealand, Pegu, Ali Masjid, South Africa 1878-9, Afghanistan 1878-80,** Tel-el-Kebir, Egypt 1882, Nile 1884-5, Suakin 1885, **Burma 1885-87, Modder River, Paardeberg, Relief of Ladysmith, South Africa 1899-1902.**

The Great War– **Mons, Le Cateau,** Retreat from Mons, Marne 1914, 18, **Aisne 1914, 18,** La Bassee 1914, **Messines 1914, 17, 18,** Armentieres 1914, **Ypres 1914, 15, 17, 18,** Hill 60, Gravenstafel, St Julien, Frezenberg, Bellewaarde, **Hooge 1915,** Loos, Mount Sorrel, **Somme 1916, 18, Albert 1916, 18,** Bazentin, Delville Wood, Pozieres, Guillemont, Flers Courcelette, Morval, Le Transloy, Ancre Heights, Ancre 1916, 18, Bapaume 1917, 18, **Arras 1917, 18,** Vimy 1917, Scarpe 1917, 18, Arleux, Hill 70, Pilckem, Langemarck 1917, Menin Road, Polygon Wood, Broodseinde, Poelcappelle, **Passchendaele, Cambrai 1917, 18,** St Quentin, Rosieres, Avre, Lys, Estaires, Hazebrouck, Bailleul, Kemmel, Bethune, Scherpenberg, Marne 1918, Soissonnais-Ourcq, Tardenois, Amiens, Drocourt Queant, Bligny, Hindenburg Line, **Havrincourt,** Epehy, Canal du Nord, St Quentin Canal, Beaurevoir, Courtrai, Selle, Valenciennes, Sambre, France and Flanders 1914-18, Piave, Vittorio Veneto, Italy 1917-18, Struma, **Doiran 1917, 18,** Macedonia 1915-18, Suvla, Landing at Suvla, Scimitar Hill, Gallipoli 1915, Rumani, Egypt 1915-17, Gaza, El Mughar, Nebi Samwil **Jerusalem,** Jericho, Tell'Asur, Megiddo, Sharon, **Palestine 1917-18, Tigris 1916,** Sharquat, Mesopotamia 1916-18, NW Frontier India 1915, 16-17, Aden, Archangel 1918-19.

Afghanistan 1919

The Second World War– Kvam, **Norway 1940,** Dyle, Defence of Escaut, Arras counter attack, St Omer-La Bassee, **Dunkirk 1940, Normandy Landing,** Villers Bocage, Tilly sur Seulles, Odon, **Fontenay le Pesnil,** Cheux, Defence of Rauray, Caen, **Hill 112,** Bourgebus Ridge, Cagny, Troarn, Mont Pincon, Souleuvre, Le Perier Ridge, St Pierre La Vielle, Noireau Crossing, Falaise, Seine 1944, Antwerp, Hechel, **Gheel,** Nederrijn, Le Havre, Antwerp-Turnhout Canal, Lower Maas, Opheusden, Venraij, Geilenkirchen, Venlo Pocket, Roer, Rhineland, Cleve, Goch, Hochwald, Xanten, Rhine, Ibbenburen, Lingen, Aller, Bremen, **North-West Europe 1940, 44-45,** Syria 1941, Halfaya 1941, Tobruk 1941, Relief of Tobruk, Gazala, Gabr el Fachri, Zt El Mrasses, Mersa Matruh, Point 174, **El Alamein, Mareth,** Sedjenane, Mine de Sedjenane, El Kourzia, **Argoub Sellah,** Medjez Plain, Gueriat el Atach Ridge, Si Abdallah, Tunis, Djebel Bou Aoukaz 1943, North Africa 1940-43, Landing in Sicily, Solarino, **Primosole Bridge, Sicily 1943, Salerno,** Salerno Hills, Cava di Tirreni, Volturno Crossing, Monte Camino, Garigliano Crossing, Minturno, Monte Tuga, **Anzio,** Campoleone, Carroceto, **Cassino II,** Trasimene Line, Arezzo, Advance to Florence, Incontro, Gothic Line, Gemmano Ridge, Carpineta, Capture of Forli, Cosina Canal Crossing, Defence of Lamone Bridgehead, Pergola Ridge, Rimini Line, Cesena, Monte Ceco, Monte Grande, Sillaro Crossing, **Italy 1943-45,** Athens, Greece 1944-45, Cos, Middle East 1942, Sittang 1942, Donbaik, **North Arakan,** Buthidaung, Ngakyedauk Pass, **Kohima,** Mandalay, **Burma 1942, 43-45.**

Kowang-San, Hill 227, **Korea 1951-53.**

Those shown in bold type are borne on The Colours.

119

Her Majesty Queen Elizabeth The Queen Mother.
Colonel-in-Chief, The Light Infantry.

120

THE REGIMENT
1997

Colonel-in-Chief
H.M. QUEEN ELIZABETH THE QUEEN MOTHER

Deputy Colonel-in-Chief
H.R.H. Princess Alexandra, the Hon. Lady Ogilvy, GCVO

Colonel
Major-General M. D. Regan, OBE

Deputy Colonels:

Durham	Colonel R. V. Brims, OBE
Shropshire & Herefordshire	Lieutenant Colonel J. K. Marsham, OBE
Somerset & Cornwall	Major-General J. F. Deverell, OBE
Yorkshire	Colonel C. M. G. Elcomb, OBE

Honorary Colonels:

5th Battalion	Colonel Sir Thomas Dunne, KCVO, K St J, JP
6th Battalion	Major-General B. M. Lane, CB, OBE
	Colonel R. W. Potts, TD, JP
7th Battalion	Colonel W. P. Catesby
8th Battalion	Colonel J. Lyles, CBE, JP

Battalions:

1st Battalion The Light Infantry	– Lt Colonel T. J. Gregson, MBE, Meeanee Barracks, Colchester CO2 7ST
2nd Battalion The Light Infantry	– Lt Colonel B. W. Barry, Alanbrooke Barracks, BFPO 16
5th Battalion The (Shropshire & Herefordshire) Light Infantry	– Lt Colonel A. M. W. Mortimer, MBE, Battalion HQ, Copthorne Barracks, Shrewsbury, Shropshire SY3 8LZ
6th Battalion The (Somerset & Cornwall) Light Infantry	– Lt Colonel A. Amber, MBE, TA Centre, Upper Bristol Road, Bath, Somerset BA1 3AF
7th Battalion The (Durham) Light Infantry	– Lt Colonel R. C. Lloyd-Williams, The Gilesgate Armoury, Gilesgate, Durham DH1 1JR
8th Battalion The (Yorkshire) Light Infantry	– Lt Colonel R. M. J. Rollo-Walker, TA Centre, George Street, Wakefield, W. Yorkshire WF1 1DW

Regimental Headquarters:
Lt Colonel P. J. Wykeham
Regimental Secretary (Extn. 5129)

Major D. H. Lawrence
Assistant Regimental Secretary (Finance) (Extn. 5130)

Major R. S. Cross
Assistant Regimental Secretary (Museum/Archives) (Extn. 5130)

Mrs. Lesley Skeet
Administrative Officer (Extn. 5127)

Light Infantry Museum (Extn. 5150).
Light Infantry Archives (Extn. 5130).
Peninsula Barracks, Romsey Road,
Winchester, Hants, SO23 8TS.
Tel: 01962 8285 plus last 2 numbers of Extn.
Fax: 01962 828500/828538

Light Infantry Offices:

Cornwall	Major R. Vyvyan-Robinson, MBE, Light Infantry Office (Cornwall), The Keep, The Barracks, Bodmin, Cornwall PL31 1EG. Tel: 01208 72810
Durham	Major D. A. Bower, Light Infantry Office (Durham), Elvet Waterside, Durham City, Co. Durham DH1 3BW. Tel: 0191 3865496
Shropshire & Herefordshire	Major J. H. H. York, MBE, BA, Light Infantry Office (Shropshire & Herefordshire), Copthorne Barracks, Shrewsbury, Shropshire SY3 8LZ. (Military 746-2425) Tel: 01743 262425/262430
Somerset	Brigadier A. I. H. Fyfe, Light Infantry Office (Somerset), 14 Mount Street, Taunton, Somerset TA1 3QE. Tel: 01823 333434
Yorkshire	Major C. M. J. Deedes, Light Infantry Office (Yorkshire), Minden House, Wakefield Road, Pontefract, Yorkshire WF8 4ES Tel: 01977 703181

ALLIANCES

Canadian Armed Forces	The Royal Hamilton Light Infantry (The Wentworth Regiment), The Armouries, Hamilton, Ontario L8R 2L1
	The North Saskatchewan Regiment, Sgt Hugh Cairns VC Armoury, 930 Idylwyld Drive North, Saskatoon, Saskatchewan S7L 0Z6
	Le Regiment de Maisonneuve, 691 Cathcart Street, Montreal, Quebec H3B 1M6
New Zealand Army	2nd Battalion (Canterbury Nelson Marlborough and West Coast) Royal New Zealand Infantry Regiment
Pakistan Army	11th Battalion The Baluch Regiment 1st Battalion The Sind Regiment
Kenya Army	1st Battalion The Kenya Rifles
Mauritius	The Mauritius Special Mobile Force
Australian Military Forces	Monash University Regiment
South African Army	The Rand Light Infantry

BONDS OF FRIENDSHIP

Royal Navy	H.M.S. INVINCIBLE H.M.S. CORNWALL

ARMY CADET FORCES
The Cornwall Cadet Battalion
The Somerset Cadet Battalion
The Royal Alderney Militia
Avon Army Cadet Force
The Herefordshire Cadet Battalion
Shropshire Army Cadet Force
Yorkshire Cadet Battalion
Durham Cadet Battalion
Cleveland Army Cadet Force
Humberside & S Yorks ACF (Doncaster Det)

COMBINED CADET FORCES
Kings College, Taunton
Taunton School, Taunton
King Edward's School, Bath
Monkton Combe School, Nr Bath
Malvern College
Prior Park College, Bath
Wells Cathedral School, Wells
Adams Grammar School, Newport
Ellesmere College, Ellesmere
Shrewsbury School, Shrewsbury
Wrekin College, Telford
6th Form College, Shrewsbury
Herefordshire Cathedral School, Hereford
Batley Grammar School, Batley
Barnard Castle School, Barnard Castle
Durham School, Durham
Wellington School

CIVIC PRIVILEGES
County Borough of Bodmin
City of Bath
City of Wells
Borough of Taunton Deane
City of Truro
City of Leeds
City of Wakefield
Borough of Batley
County Borough of Doncaster
Borough of Pontefract
Borough of Wear Valley

Borough of Shrewsbury
Borough of Bridgnorth
City of Hereford
Borough of Oswestry
Borough of Wenlock
Borough of Ludlow
City of Durham
City of Sunderland
Borough of Hartlepool
Borough of Stockton
Borough of Darlington

Tidworth – 31 May 1991

Major Basil Jones, a regular officer, was Second in Command of the battalion until he went into hospital with polio in Tehran, when we were stationed in Persia, in 1942. He recovered, and after the War retired with the rank of Lieutenant Colonel, with his wife, to the South of England. I met him in Cheshire on a number of occasions until he died in 1967.

His son, Peter Jones, was in the Regiment, and we became close friends when both our families lived in Heswall, Wirral, Cheshire after the War. We attended many Regimental Reunions together in Liverpool, Leeds and London, and I became godfather to their second daughter.

The photograph of him (see next page) was taken at Tidworth, when we, and our wives, attended the Presentation of the Colours to the First, Second and Third Battalions The Light Infantry by Her Majesty Queen Elizabeth The Queen Mother in May 1991. He has retired and lives with his wife in Gloucestershire.

Captain Peter Jones KOYLI.

Regimental Reunions

When the Regiment was disbanded into The Light Infantry Regiment, and we became the Second Battalion The Light Infantry in 1969, I attended a service in the KOYLI chapel at York Minster, which was conducted by Lt. Col. A.F. McRiggs (Raggs) who became ordained after the War in about 1962. He was formerly my Company Commander during the War, and later commanded the battalion in Sicily after Lt. Col. A.F.S. Douglas was wounded, and was in command at the time of my capture by the Germans. The colours were laid down in the chapel. The service was attended by many members of the Regiment and their wives, and we had a happy gathering for lunch afterwards in the Old Hall near the Minster. I maintained contact with 'Raggs' and his family for many years. He died in 1977, aged eighty-eight.

Every year near the day we set sail from Liverpool in March 1942, the Signals Section organize an annual reunion of the 1st Bn KOYLI 1939–1945 to which the officers are invited. I have attended a number of these at The Griffin Hotel, Leeds.

In June each year the Regimental Officers Club have their Annual Reunion in Claridges Hotel, London, attended by past and present officers. I attended two luncheons when Her Majesty Queen Elizabeth The Queen Mother was present. The first was in June 1979, and the second with my wife in 1987. On both occasions about 100 officers and their wives were present, and it was a day to remember being presented to The Queen Mother, our Colonel-in-Chief.

1st Battalion KOYLI Reunion – Griffin Hotel, Leeds, 1994.
Captain J.R.M. Newsome, Sergeant John Megson.

The photograph above shows myself and my sergeant at a luncheon in Leeds. He is now eighty years of age, and was with me until India, when he went into hospital with severe dysentery. He was unable to rejoin the battalion and I met him again after the War.

1st Battalion KOYLI Reunion – Griffin Hotel, Leeds, May 1996.
Major C.M. Deedes, Regimental Secretary,
Captain J.R.M. Newsome.

*Remember the brave men
who waded ashore in Sicily
55 years ago, the very first
soldiers of democracy to breach
the walls of Nazi Europe.*